Rapid Automated Prototyping:

An Introduction

Rapid Automated Prototyping:

An Introduction

by Lamont Wood

Industrial Press Inc.

New York

Library of Congress Cataloging-in-Publication Data

Wood, Lamont, 1953–
    Rapid automated prototyping : an introduction / by Lamont Wood.
        160 p.   15.2 x 23.5 cm.
    Includes index.
    ISBN 0-8311-3047-4
    1. Prototypes, Engineering.   2. Computer-aided design.   I. Title.
TS171.4.W66   1993
620' .004'0385—dc20   92-43482
                                                                            CIP

Industrial Press Inc.
200 Madison Avenue
New York, NY 10016-4078

First Edition

Printed & bound by Edwards Brothers, Ann Arbor, Michigan from Postscript files prepared by KP Company, Brooklyn, New York.

1   2   3   4   5

Contents

To my father, Roy G. Wood, who gave me that Erector set when I was little.

I would like to thank all the users and vendors interviewed for this book and also Terry Wohlers of Wohlers and Associates, Fort Collins, CO.

Trademarks

CIBATOOL is a registered trademark of Ciba-Geigy Corp.

Cubital and Solider are registered trademarks; and Solimer, Soliwax, and Solitone are trademarks of Cubital Ltd.

DeSolite and SLR are registered trademarks of DSM Desotech Inc.

Echo and Plexus are trademarks of Cyberware Laboratory Inc.

EXactomer is a trademark of Allied-Signal Inc.

Loctite is a registered trademark of Loctite Corporation.

LOM and LAMINATED OBJECT MANUFACTURING are registered trademarks of Helisys Inc.

Selective Laser Sintering, SLS, and Sinterstation 2000 are trademarks of DTM Corp.

SLA, SLA-250, and SLA-500 are trademarks of 3D Systems Inc.

Soliform is a trademark of Tejin Seiki Co. Ltd.

SOMOS is a trademark of E. I. du Pont de Nemours & Co.

STEREOS is a trademark of EOS GmbH.

Stratasys, 3D-MODELER, FDM, and ProtoSlice are trademarks of Stratasys Inc.

Surveyor and DataSculpt are registered trademarks of Laser Design Inc.

All other trademarks are recognized.

Introduction 1

Rapid automated prototyping is a field so new that it does not have an accepted name (despite the one we just used). Toolless model-making, automated fabrication, rapid prototyping, and desktop manufacturing are a few of the designations used.

Fortunately, they all mean the same thing — the creation of three-dimensional objects directly from CAD files, without human intervention. You input a CAD file, wait a few hours, and out pops (so to speak) a model of the object. Unlike numerical-control (NC) tooling, the model is created by adding material instead of cutting it away from a solid block. Therefore, complex shapes are no more trouble to create than are simple cubes.

Notice, however, that we said that what you get from the machine is a model — not usually an end-user item. This new technology is used for prototyping, not actual production, at least, as we will see, for the moment.

Current Applications

Prototypes are integral to the industrial design cycle, for any of these three purposes:

★ **Aesthetic visualization** — to see what the thing looks like, especially a consumer item that must look appealing when painted and packaged. Promotional models, models for business presentations, and architectural models fall in this area.

* **Form-fit-and-function testing** — to make sure the part fits to and works with the other parts to which it is intended to be attached.
* **Casting models** — to make a casting mold around the part for full-scale production of replicas of the part.

However, conventional model-making methods can require weeks (for moderately complicated items) to months (for complex ones). If tests of the model lead to design changes, a new model will be needed for further tests. Indeed, a new one may be needed for each iteration of the design cycle.

With rapid automated prototyping, however, turnaround for the model-making step can be cut to days, and the model itself can often be made overnight — a compelling advantage at a time when the global nature of the industrial marketplace makes minimizing time-to-market cycle times and maximizing productivity a matter of corporate life and death.

Additionally, with rapid prototyping, users report they have been able to cut out a step in the product design cycle — they can skip soft tooling and prove a design using rapid prototyping models. They can then go direct to hard tooling, or they can even make casting molds from the rapid prototyping model.

Thus, it is no surprise that rapid prototyping has been the subject of an increasing number of management seminars and colloquiums. It has been widely adopted in the automotive field, and other uses are as varied as crafting custom bone implants to making Hollywood movie props.

This book will give the user a broad overview of what constitutes the world of rapid automated prototyping, in terms of what technologies were being marketed and used in North America as of late 1992, with input from actual users when available. (Only obviously viable, commercially available systems were examined. No attempt has been made to look into all rapid prototyping development efforts in the academic and corporate worlds. At least two such commercial efforts foundered or aborted while this book was in preparation.)

Basically, the reader will encounter a technology on the cusp — its enormous potential is obvious, but reaching that potential is fraught with practical difficulties. It is foreseeable that rapid prototyping could become the engineering version of desktop publishing. Remember that, with the right desktop publishing software and a laser printer, any office can produce a facsimile of the printed page that can serve the purpose as well as a typeset and printed document would. Similarly, perhaps, someday with rapid prototyping any engineering office could output CAD files to a model-making machine, and they would doubtless find that these models could be made to serve many purposes.

If rapid prototyping can move beyond model-making, rapid automated prototyping could be the dawn of a new industrial revolution, with fully computerized manufacturing firms able to produce any end-user item on demand, from any automated fabrication machine located anywhere. The concepts of inventory and shipping could become obsolete. Intellectual property — the copyrighted CAD files from which end-user items are produced under royalty, and their brand names — will become the only industrial property worth owning. The firms that produce those designs for those brands may themselves produce nothing tangible and own nothing tangible except perhaps for the buildings that house their design teams.

If, however, the practicalities are not overcome, rapid prototyping may languish as a niche technology — a fancy toy for design engineers.

It is difficult to say at this point which way things will move and at what speed. The practical considerations themselves, however, can be clearly distinguished. They are part tolerances, model sizes, materials, software, and prices.

Tolerances

Tolerances on parts produced in rapid prototyping machines today average in the range of five-thousandths of an inch. Skilled users of the 3D Systems stereolithography systems report getting tolerances of one-thousandths for small parts. (So say the users questioned for this book.

Tolerances reported by the vendors are expressed in various ways, including thousandths per inch and overall percentages, meaning tolerances can be fine for small parts but loose for large ones.)

Whether such tolerances are good or bad depend heavily on what the users are doing with the prototypes. Those interested in aesthetic visualization are normally quite pleased, except that they might have to paint the models. Those interested in form-fit-and-function testing report that they may have to machine critical surfaces and that some models are more durable than others. Those who want to make casting tools directly from the prototypes also say they have to do postfinishing. Other users note that their production castings may have no better tolerances than the prototypes and so refuse to get excited.

Some users, however, demand at least half a thousandth of an inch tolerances. At this point, they must either postfinish the models with skilled craftspeople or use some other model-making method. For the universal adoption of rapid prototyping, therefore, tolerances must be improved by about an order of magnitude.

Model Sizes

One automotive engineer said that when he presented his department vice president with the idea of a rapid automated prototyping machine, the first thing the executive asked was, "When can we build a whole car with one?".

Indeed, model size, users report, seems to be a consistent concern with management. The engineers actually using the machines, however, report that the working "envelope" of most model-making machines (which today average about a cubic foot) is enough for the vast majority of the parts they make. Larger parts can be made in sections and then glued together — a task that does not daunt skilled model-makers.

Therefore, while it might appear to be one, size capacities are not an overriding issue for prototyping. For making end-user items, though, capacities will probably have to be increased.

Materials

While tolerances and model sizes can be expected to improve in the future, the question is cloudier with materials. To produce a working hard-metal part (a crank shaft, for instance) through rapid automated prototyping does not look promising for the near future.

The most widespread form of rapid prototyping is stereolithography (described in Chapter 2), which depends on the polymerization of liquid resins. The resulting prototypes, therefore, are plastic models whose strength and elasticity depend on the properties of the resin that was used and the thoroughness of the postprocess curing that was performed. If a plastic part is being prototyped, the stereolithography part may be comfortably close to the final product, in properties as well as appearance. If a titanium steel part is being prototyped, the appearance may be close (especially after finishing and painting), but its properties will not be in the same ball park.

Users report, however, that casting foundries have been able, by experimenting with the parameters of "dewaxing," to use stereolithography models for investment casting.

Other model-making technologies described in this book produce plastic or plywood-like objects — except "Selective Laser Sintering"™ (described in Chapter 3.) Selective laser sintering can produce parts in investment casting wax, nylon, and plastic, and there has been development work in ceramics and low-temperature metals such as copper, but steel is a long way off.

Therefore, it appears that "manufacturing on demand" of end-user items such as cars is not on the immediate horizon, but the technology in this field is so new that its true potential or limitations cannot yet be discerned.

Software

Adequate use of rapid automated prototyping technology nearly always requires the use of solid-modeling CAD (as explained in Chapter

7). Just a few years ago, this consideration was thought to be an obstacle to the spread of the new technology, since even major corporations were still using two-dimensional CAD and shrank from converting their operations. Indeed, model-making service bureaus reported getting designs scrawled on the back of stained cocktail napkins.

Today, the majority of users do seem to be using solid-modeling, or at least three-dimensional surface-modeling, CAD. The conversion has been made.

Fortunately, the rapid prototyping industry early on standardized on an interface between CAD software and model-making machines, called the .STL format (described in Chapter 7). Using a three-dimensional CAD package that produces .STL output, you can be confident that what you have created on the screen can be turned into a solid object, possibly overnight. (CAD packages supporting .STL are listed in Chapter 7.) The only caveat is that there may still be a learning curve with a particular process, in terms of how to position the object in the model-maker, how to allow for shrinkage (if any), and where and how to added temporary structural supports (if needed).

Software, however, remains an issue for individual users who may still be using two-dimensional drafting. Sources stress that users should approach software from the standpoint of integrating all aspects of their design efforts, so as to promote "concurrent engineering," with engineering, designing, analysis, and documentation happening at the same time. Rapid automated prototyping, from this viewpoint, is just one more piece of a mosaic that is held together by software.

Price

Many users observed that, if rapid prototyping machines cost no more than laser printers, there would probably be one in every engineering office. Unfortunately, they can cost several hundred thousand dollars. Of course, the original laser printers were also bulky, expensive monsters, but, as the market grew, quantity production became possible, and the recovery of the initial development costs was no longer an issue.

Whether that cycle will occur in rapid prototyping machines remains to be seen.

Conclusions

The rapid automated prototyping field would seem to be in about the same position that the microcomputer field was in about 1979. Various models had come out and pioneering users had found ways to employ them. Their potential was obvious and whetted the appetites of many potential users, but those same potential users recoiled from the adventure of actually adopting microcomputers. Then, IBM came out in 1981 with a model to which others standardized, the market soared, prices fell, there were repeated market shake-outs, and competition forced the surviving vendors to improve price-performance almost exponentially. Today, one sees businesses literally built around microcomputers.

Such a rate of change is not likely in the rapid prototyping field, if only because the final output is solid objects rather than intangible data, but the 1979 parallel is still there. Alternate approaches are emerging. Pioneering users have gotten involved. Other potential users have had their appetites whetted. Standardization, shake-outs, a fevered market, and intense development efforts remain to be seen. Admittedly, they may never be seen, but, chances are, they will — and this book will form the first pages of a very exciting history.

Stereolithography Systems 2

Stereolithography prototyping systems depend on the use of photoreactive polymers, usually ones that react to ultraviolet (UV) light. When struck by sufficient UV light, the resin solidifies (polymerizes). Therefore, by selectively shining UV light onto the surface of a vat of such a polymer, one could form one layer (slice) of a model. The light can take the form of a precisely directly laser beam (the approach taken by 3D Systems and others) or a floodlight directed through an optical mask (the approach taken by Cubital®).

To make the next and subsequent layers, the object can either be dipped slightly deeper into a vat of the polymer (the approach taken by 3D Systems and others), or a new film of liquid polymer can be spread atop the growing model (the approach taken by Cubital).

Whatever the approach, the resulting models are limited to polymer resins, disappointing those who would prefer models made from production material or investment casting wax (although people have experimented with using them for investment casting). However, a wide range of stereolithography resins has reached the market, and they will be covered later in the chapter. Further advances in resin technology can be expected.

3D SYSTEMS INC.
26081 Avenue Hall
Valencia, CA 91355
805-295-5600
fax: 805-257-1200

3D Systems was founded in March 1986 in San Gabriel, CA, by Charles Hull and Raymond Freed. Freed, chairman and CEO, was a businessman in the electronic component field.

Hull, the president of the new firm, had conceived the idea of stereolithography in September 1982 while working as vice president of a San Gabriel firm call UVP Inc., which specialized in products that involved UV light. Some of these used UV-cured inks and coatings. Hull, who had formerly worked as a design engineer, was familiar with the problems associated with plastic products and tooling, so he began examining the UV-curable materials to develop a prototyping method for plastic products. No special polymer was developed for the purpose — he recalls simply trying about 100 different polymer resins before finding one that would work.

Hull had finished the first feasibility machine in February 1983 and applied for a basic patent in August 1984. Money was raised for 3D Systems after acquiring the exclusive rights to the UVP Inc. stereolithography technology in May 1986. The firm's first product, the SLA-1, began shipping in early 1988, and, in July 1988, the chemical firm, Ciba-Geigy, bought 37.5 percent of 3D, after first signing a joint polymer research agreement with the firm. (The public owns 36 percent, and the founders own the remaining 26.5 percent.) The firm began making a profit in the third quarter of 1989.

"There are a lot of ways to do prototyping, and we have done a lot of research and development in other ways (besides stereolithography)," Hull said. "I am sure we will be concentrating more on the applications than on the technology of how to get there. Currently we use photoreactive systems, and we are continually amazed by its flexibility and the users' ability to take that technology into different applications. At this point we don't see any stumbling blocks in the technology — we have not pressed its limits in terms of accuracy or speed.

"We are not visionaries saying we are going to change the world," added Hull. "We are focusing on the interface between design and manufacturing, since that is the major bottleneck in the industrial world. A lot of work has been done to automate design and production, but there is still this craft-oriented world in between, and we see a need to bring automatic tools into that area. In the end, in the big picture, it may be called a revolution."

In late 1992, the firm had sold about 300 SLA™ machines worldwide — making it the leading rapid automated prototyping systems supplier by far — and was offering three different models.

SLA-500™
Announced: 1990 (See Figure 2-1)
Laser: Argon ion
Model Size: 20 x 20 x 24 inches
Resolution: +/- 0.005 inch
Price: $385,000.00

Touted as being five to ten times faster than the SLA-250™ because of its more powerful laser, the SLA-500 comes with a Silicon Graphics workstation running 3D's slicing software.

SLA-250™
Announced: 1988 (See Figure 2-2)
Laser: Helium Cadmium
Model Size: 10 x 10 x 10 inches
Resolution: +/- 0.005 inch
Price: $185,000.00

The SLA-250 was 3D's second-generation machine, replacing its original SLA-1. A workstation is an extra-cost option, costing about $30,000.00 to $40,000.00 with the 3D slicing software.

SLA-190™
Announced: 1990 (See Figure 2-3)
Laser: Helium Cadmium
Model Size: 7.5 x 7.5 x 9 inches
Resolution: +/- 0.005 inch
Price: $95,000.00

Figure 2-1. 3D Systems' SLA-500 stereolithography model-making machine, with a working envelope of 20 x 20 x 24 inches.

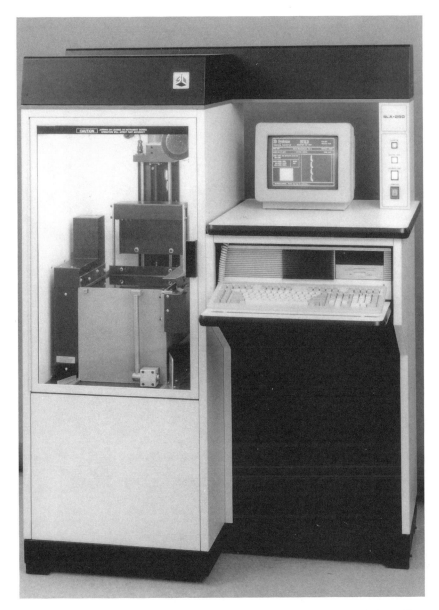

Figure 2-2. 3D Systems' SLA-250 stereolithography model-making machine, with a working envelope of 10 x 10 x 10 inches.

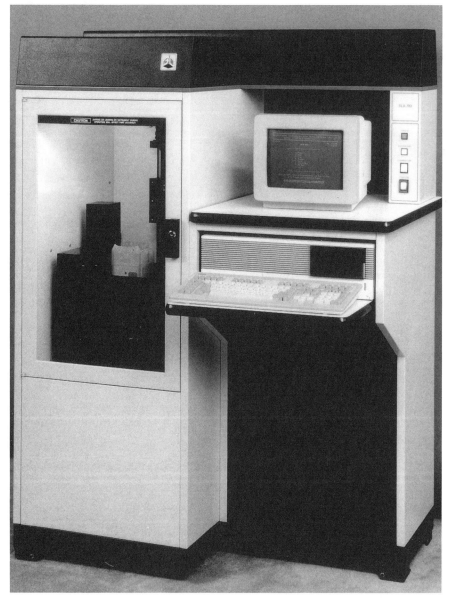

Figure 2-3. 3D Systems' SLA-190 stereolithography model-making machine, with a working envelope of 7.5 x 7.5 x 9 inches.

Although it is now 3D's introductory system, the SLA-190 was actually introduced after its SLA-500. A workstation is an extra-cost option, priced between $30,000.00 and $40,000.00 with the 3D slicing software. It uses a resin with a lower viscosity than the other machines, since there is no blade to spread the resin for each new layer after the part elevator is lowered.

All three machines use the same basic approach: the top of a vat of liquid polymer resin is scanned with a UV laser, and the hardened polymer forms one cross-section or slice of the model. The "elevator" that the part rests on is then lowered slightly into the vat, and the next layer is scanned and hardened, adhering to the previous layer. The entire cross-section of an object must be scanned so that it is filled in solid — simply outlining the perimeter is not enough.

Since cross-sections of an overhanging part might form unconnected islands that would float away during the process, webbing and supports have to be added to the computer-aided design (CAD) file before model-making begins.

After the model is completed, the unused resin is poured out, and the item is cured by exposure to intense UV light or heat. Some warping and shrinking takes place at this step, but experienced users report that it can be allowed for at the design stage. (See Figures 2-4 and 2-5 for the appearance of finished parts.)

Materials

3D offers several resins produced by Ciba-Geigy. These are available exclusively from 3D. Information on them is contained in the Resin Vendors section later in the chapter.

Software

3D's workstation software performs slicing only. The .STL format was developed for 3D's machine, and its software, of course, supports .STL data files. 3D's software can also spot and correct minor flaws in .STL files, such as missing or overlapping facets.

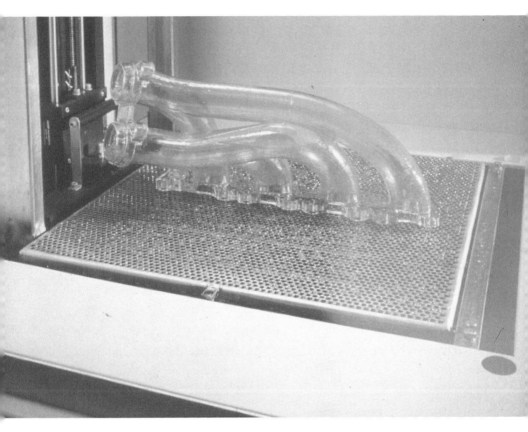

Figure 2-4. Prototype of a manifold made with a 3D Systems stereolithography model-making machine.

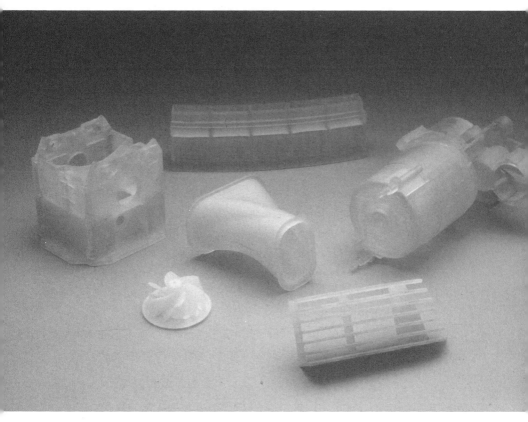

Figure 2-5. Miscellaneous parts produced by a 3D Systems stereolithography model-making machine.

A CATIA (IBM CAD) interface has also been recently released. Since it is based on cutting tool paths instead of tiny triangular surface facets like .STL, the CATIA interface is considered superior for creating curved surfaces. 3D has also announced its intention to develop an IGES interface.

The latest versions of 3D's workstation software gives the same interface to all three systems, simplifying training. 3D has also begun selling the software separately from the hardware, for $15,000.00

Note on Quadrax

Quadrax Laser Technologies Inc. of Portsmouth, RI, had previously marketed a stereolithography machine, called the Mark 1000 Laser Modeling System, featuring a higher-power Argon laser with a controllable beam diameter. (The beam's spot on the surface of the resin could be 0.0035 to 0.125 inch in diameter, using a three-mirror focusing system.) After patent litigation with 3D Systems, Quadrax agreed in early 1992 to stop selling the machine and trade the technology it had developed to 3D Systems in exchange for 3D common stock. Therefore, Quadrax's technology may be expected to turn up in future 3D Systems SLA machines.

Customer Reactions

Owner of a model-making shop in the Midwest

We have made small parts with an accuracy of plus or minus one thousandth, but I tell the customers plus or minus five — that's about as accurate as plastic injection molding. People seem to have greater expectations from the modeling machine than from the molding machine — they want accuracy of within a thousandth or two. I have compared parts from customers and found that they could not hold the accuracy in manufacturing that we hold in the SLA machine, so expectations may be a little out of line. But, of course, from a service bureau you demand higher tolerances, just as you would expect no mismatches if you have a professional wallpaper your home.

We have an SLA–250 that runs 19 to 20 hours a day, seven days a week. I do all my own maintenance. I have noticed that people who have problems with these machines are people who are not in the tooling field and may be intimidated by the fact that there are mechanical parts in it. We're used to taking complicated things apart.

We bought the machine in November 1988, and we are on our ninth laser. If you buy a laser new they cost about $10,000.00 It takes about an hour and a half to change one. The machine was converted to an SLA–250 from an SLA–1.

Since 1988, the materials have changed — there is a greater variety of resins, and they are much better. We used one called EXactomer™ from Allied Signal. We think it's better than anything on the market — there's less shrinkage, greater green strength, and the lower viscosity lets you build smaller details easier. But, keep in mind that there are things that we look for in a resin that a manufacturer would not want. I look for a resin that is not brittle, but rigid enough to cast or make spray-metal tools off of. A lot of our parts are used as patterns. If I were to put some of the SLA parts, painted to look like production parts, in a box with company wrapping, you could not tell they were SLA parts. They look like manufactured parts. They don't have the weight of steel, but they are close to that of aluminum.

We use 3D's proprietary software to run the machine, with Bridge-works to put supports in for the parts. A lot of customers give us solid-model files in .STL format, and the only thing we have to do is put in support structures and build it. That's the quickest way of getting a part back to their design.

Some customers forward the (CAD) data to those (cast-making shops) building the production tools for them, and we pass along the IGES file, so several people are working simultaneously off the same database. We can modem data to subcontractors to make details, when we are pressed for time. We once had 11 subcontractors working on a job at one time.

We have made prototype injection plastic molds, involving 150 or so injection parts, from two-dimensional drawings in six days, using my people and five other shops that do good work. And design changes were made during the process. It would have taken four or five weeks previously.

The modem is the slowest link in the technology. One finished cut had seven million bytes of NC code. Typically we send tapes by overnight courier.

There is curing warpage and shrinkage, but it's like heat distortion under a grinder. If you look at a 3D Systems machine as a machine with parameters that you have to machine by, then it's an extremely functional tool. But that doesn't mean the operator can't make a mistake, as with a milling or grinding machine. Knowing how to work the machine gets us invited to a lot of parties.

I would like to see the machine have a replaceable vat, and 3D is supposed to be working on that. Now it takes a day to change resins, since you have to clean the whole machine.

There are still some customers surprised by the technology, even in awe of it, but those who have been using it for a while may take it for granted.

Engineer at a Detroit car company

Since the new resins came out for the SLA-250 we have been very happy with it — it is a lot easier to build parts and get supports off. It has been very reliable. Ours is constantly busy. Actually, it's going to be moved — it's so reliable we want to put it in a production shop. It's had only regular maintenance.

We are not happy with our SLA-500. We cannot consistently get good parts. There have been a number of mechanical breakdowns and obscure build failures. And there have been some issues with resin quality — parts have come out really soft. We have seen it lose the network connection 15 hours into a build, hiccup, and lose the whole thing. But the reliability problem may be our fault — I'm not sure how clean the power is. But our SLA-250 is in the same room and has not been affected.

Accuracy varies by hatching method and the postcure time. We were not pleased with the variability.

3D is getting its act together with the "Christmas Tree" and "Window Panes" self-diagnostic tests and finding out how the (polymerization) process really works. But, even with the diagnostics, the postcure time can have a great effect on the part accuracy. That bothered us since when you are doing it in volume you won't have time to monitor your postcure times. And sometimes you have to rotate the part to cure it right.

NC manager for a maker of computer printers on the West Coast

We do form-fit-and-function testing on printer parts and have been fairly successful in getting our preliminary testing done (with stereolithography models).

Cubital has been the second most used, after 3D. One difference has been the materials, since there is more variety with 3D. And 3D (technology) is more available, since there are a lot of service bureaus using it. It's easier to get the kind of turnaround we need.

We need 0.2 percent accuracy overall. Using a percentage figure (for accuracy) gives you more leeway on a large part. But, you have to be realistic about the process, with the shrinkage and warpage problems. If you are going to be rigid about how you are going to specify your part you might as well machine the parts. There are still some problems you have to live with.

The service bureaus can usually get 0.2 percent, but the part configuration has a lot to do with it. Many service bureaus have become proficient with difficult issues and can solve problems quickly.

(By using rapid automated prototyping for preliminary prototypes and by making production prototypes by hand) we can get the parts in the quality we need at that step of the design process. Some steps need speed, some need accuracy.

General manager of a rapid prototyping service bureau on the West Coast

We are a service bureau for rapid prototyping and were an early user of 3D Systems.

There has been a massive evolution in the resins available. At first, all that was available were the original Ciba-Geigy resins, and they were very brittle and not very forgiving for any use. We pushed hard for other resins and used outside sources as soon as they were available, first to Desotek, and since then to a newer one, the best but most expensive and the slowest to scan, (Allied-Signal's) EXactomer. It's fairly good but really slow — it takes two to four times longer to build a part. So before we could switch over we had to get a hotter laser — 40 milliwatts — to stay in business. The lasers are better now, too. You can expect them to last 2,000 hours, whereas, before, 1,000 hours was good.

We played a lot with the scanning matrix for the hatches (the crosshatching used to fill the solid areas of a slice). We also played quite a bit with designing supports. We had to figure out a lot of stuff ourselves.

One significant improvement that 3D came out with is adding a weave in the way the laser scans the solid area of the part. That was the single biggest improvement. Because of the nature of stereolithography, you build internal stresses into the part, and you can try to compensate by the way you crosshatch. It (the weave) compensates for curl, there's less warping, and the parts tend to be straighter.

Now we are getting +/- 0.002 inch tolerances. Our customers are a lot happier than they were two years ago, when we were getting closer to 5 or 6 thousandths. Ninety percent are very happy with our (2 thousandths) tolerances. Given that they want very complex parts very quickly, there is no alternative.

President of an engineering service company on the East Coast

We are an engineering service company that assists major corporations with developing new products, utilizing CAD/CAM technologies. Our focus is in three areas: CAD engineering services, stereolithography, and vacuum casting. We use CAD parametric and solid modeling software to create and modify designs of complex mechanical parts. The use of high-power CAD engineering workstations allows us to create designs and modify them quickly.

Once a design is created, the database is processed through our stereolithography process. On average, we produce an SLA model of the CAD design within 5 to 7 working days. If necessary, the process can be completed in 3 days. We call the SLA model a "touchy-feely" model because it is mainly utilized for communication and for evaluating form and fit. Its limitations come into play when an engineer wants to use the model as a functional prototype, which will be subjected to forces. Currently, the SLA resins are limited, and nine times out of ten the SLA material will not be close enough to simulate the actual material that will be used for the production part.

Model size and tolerances (in stereolithography) are a very big issue. We find that there are three major factors in producing an accurate part: preprocessing (support structure design); the SLA process settings; and postprocessing (postcuring and finishing). We have experienced technicians, toolmakers, and model makers (craftspeople) on our staff for performing our rapid prototyping functions.

Our SLA-250 produces parts (in a single run) that fall within a 10 x 10 x 10 inch envelope. An SLA-500 can produce larger parts (20 x 20 x 24 inch), however, the cost of the SLA-500 is more than twice that of the SLA-250. It is very common for us to produce larger parts by fixturing and bonding several SLA parts together. Some examples of large parts we produced are plastic bezels for microwave ovens, large castings for tractors, and computer housings. Due to the stereolithography process limitations, we find that tighter tolerances can be held by piecing together several smaller SLA parts, versus one single large part produced on an SLA-500.

Although the SLA model plays an important role in the new product development process, functional prototypes that can be tested under loads are much more important to our clients. We fill this need by hooking up the two advanced technologies of stereolithography and vacuum casting. We are providing our clients with plastic molded parts or metal castings that simulate their exact design geometry. Quantities range from 5 to 150 parts. Starting with a solid CAD file, on average we produce ten functional thermoset plastic parts within a 2- to 3-week time frame. We utilize the most advanced thermoset resins, which closely simulate production plastic materials.

Although stereolithography can produce any part geometry, we find that ideal parts for rapid prototyping are complex injection molded or casting part designs (parts with many fillets, radiuses, and draft angled walls). Parts of this complexity are not economical to produce with conventional machining, NC machining, or soft (aluminum) tooling processes.

If implemented correctly, CAD tools and rapid prototyping technologies can have a major impact on assisting the engineering process of developing new products.

We are finding that it is becoming more common for the SLA model to be utilized as a tool for communicating the design intent instead of the traditional blueprint. More importantly, I believe this new process greatly improves the quality of the design, due to the fact that it allows the engineers to go through several design iterations prior to committing to manufacturing.

Stereolithographer for a plastics firm in Eastern Canada

We started as a computer animation firm, and we found that what the clients wanted was to represent real-life objects through animation. When we came across stereolithography we said this is what clients are really looking for — three-dimensional objects instead of the animation of three-dimensional objects. The clients were using animations for marketing, to see how pieces fit together or to see how things looked on the shelf.

We were the first Canadian company to buy a 3D machine.

After having the machine (an SLA-250) for four years, we have progressed into the manufacturing business, doing prototypes and low-run production.

Our customers are satisfied with its output. We are hitting five thousandths tolerance. The machine runs constantly. We made 50 or 60 models this month.

We have learned a lot about using the machine. It's not a process where you push a button, and it's done. There is a lot of hard work behind it. But it does turn around prototypes faster than conventional methods.

We did not anticipate the amount of up-front CAD work needed. There was not the number of three-dimensional solid or fully surfaced models we see now, and we had to do a lot of redrafting into solid modeling CAD. But in the last year the situation has completely reversed, and now 80 percent of the orders are in solid model CAD.

If I have an .STL file, a 2- to 3-day turnaround is more than likely, depending on the backlog, but most jobs don't last more than 2 weeks in the shop.

But, we will apply the best technology to the job. Stereolithography was not meant for making dice — square, solid, fixed objects — but for intricate, complicated models. A perfect example of where it should be used would be a hockey player's face mask. It's complicated, has thin walls, and needs to be done fast.

Our clients find that they can sell their parts before going to heavy tooling by showing their SLA part. They can make four or five different designs, put them on the table, show their customers, and find out what is better for their market, and go to heavy tooling. And they can do that in a couple of weeks. Previously they might have to wait 6 months just to get the models made.

Part size has not been a major issue — more often than not most will fit in the 10-inch cube (of the SLA-250), or they can be sectioned. Five thousandths tolerances is quite acceptable to many clients. Or you can do a second build and adjust the shrink factor and other variables. But, more often than not, if there is something that needs higher tolerances, you can machine it.

We don't build all models in stereolithography — it's not always feasible or worth it. But, once you have your CAD data, you can go to stereolithography, or NC tooling, or finite element analysis, or computer visuals for rendering.

European and Japanese SLA "Clones"

Several firms in Europe and Japan have come out with stereolithography machines that strongly resemble the 3D SLA machines, especially in their use of lasers to polymerize liquid resin selectively. These machines have not been marketed in the United States, and 3D executives say that it is because of 3D's strong patent position. The two firms detailed below are thought to have representative systems.

EOS

EOS GmbH
Electro Optical Systems
Pasinger St. 2
D-8033 Planegg/München
Germany
089-8991310
fax: 089-8598402

EOS was founded in 1989 by industrial laser specialists in an effort to achieve a fully integrated prototyping system. The resulting product includes both a model-making machine and a scanner. The scanner can be used to check the accuracy of a part from the model-making machine or to "reverse engineer" an existing part or model.

STEREOS™ 400

Size: 252 x 145 x 198 cm, 800 kg
Model Size: 400 x 400 x 250 mm
Vat Capacity: 70 liters
Laser: 100 mW Argon ion
Laser Beam: 0.15 mm
Accuracy: +/- 0.05 mm

STEREOS 600

Size: 180 x 220 x 220 cm, 1300 kg
Model Size: 600 x 600 x 400 mm
Vat Capacity: 230 liters
Laser: 100 or 200 mW Argon ion
Laser Beam: 0.15 mm
Accuracy: +/- 0.05 mm

Both systems feature interchangeable resin vats that allow the resin to be changed quickly. EOS literature also mentioned vats as small as 2 liters to let the users experiment or make small parts without committing large volumes of resin.

Various lasers other than the ones listed can be used. More powerful ones may require water cooling.

In an effort to ensure an equally tight focus throughout the entire bottom of the work area, the laser beam is focused through a flat-field lens after being bounced off the aiming mirror. The beam moves at up to 10 meters per second.

EOS estimates that its STEREOS 400 is about a third faster than the 3D SLA-500 and much faster than the SLA-250. (Assuming a full-size car manifold: 100 hours for the SLA-250, 254 hours for the SLA-500, and 15 hours for the EOS 400, states the firm's literature.)

Two workstations are used, a "slice computer" to process the CAD files and a "process computer" to run the model-making machine. The slice computer is described as a 32-bit RISC Unix workstation running X-Windows, with an Ethernet and a tape drive interface. The process computer is a 486 PC running Windows.

EOSCAN 100
Measurement Area (X–Y): 100 x 70 mm
Range (Z): 30 mm
Resolution: 0.02 mm
Maximum Surface Slope: 43°

EOSCAN 250
Measurement Area (X–Y): 250 x 200 mm
Range (Z): 120 mm
Resolution: 0.02 mm
Measurement Error: 0.1 mm
Maximum Surface Slope: 45°
Maximum Object Size: 400 x 400 x 250 mm

EOSCAN represents a video-based optical measurement system, using the projection moiré principle. A grid of fine parallel lines is projected onto the target object. When observed at the correct angle through a reference grating, moiré interference patterns appear, corresponding to surface height contours. The video image is processed by the 486 PC to derive three-dimensional data points.

Software

Files in the .STL, CATIA, VDA-FS, and IGES formats can be used. The slice workstation runs under OSF Motif.

Materials

EOS uses the DuPont line of SOMOS line of photopolymers. See the Resin Vendors section later in this chapter for details. Any UV-sensitive photo-reactive polymer resin can be used, however, as long as it is compatible with argon ion lasers.

TEIJIN SEIKI CO. LTD.
Opto Marketing Division
Shinjuku NS Building, 4-1, 2-Chome
Nishi-Shinjuku, Shinjuku-Ku
Tokyo 163-08
Japan
81-3-3348-2185
fax: 81-3-3348-1050
telex: 2325162 TSEIKI J

(Tokyo being what it is, Teijin Seiki supplies a map to the Shinjuku NS Building in the Nishi-Shinjuku area, off Kosho-Kaido Avenue, closely bounded by the Shinjuku Washington Hotel, the KDD Building, and the Tokyo Metropolitan Government Building Number Two.)

Teijin Seiki's offering is called the Soliform™ Solid Forming System, using an argon ion laser and a slightly larger model size than the SLA-250.

Soliform Solid Forming System
Machine Size: 7 feet x 8 feet 9 inches x 2 feet 6 inches
Model Size: 12 x 12 x 12 inches
Accuracy: X axis: 0.002 inch per inch
         Y axis: 0.002 inch per inch
         Z axis: 0.006 inch per inch
Layer Thickness: 0.005 to 0.02 inch
Layer Formation: 2 minutes average, 7 maximum

Materials

The Soliform machine uses Dupont's SOMOS 2100 and 3100 photoreactive polymer resins, described in the Resin Vendors section later in this chapter.

Software

The Soliform machine uses a Unix workstation (apparently a Sun) running graphical software under X-Windows. Input is via .STL files, ASCII or binary.

Other Vendors

Sony, Mitsubishi, and Mitsui are all reported to be offering stereolithography machines in Japan, but have not marketed them in the United States. Reportedly, the main difference from the 3D SLA machines is shown by the Mitsubishi machine, which uses an X–Y plotter arm to position the mirror, instead of flickering it with a galvanometer.

CUBITAL AMERICA INC.
1307F Allen Road
Troy, MI 48083
313-585-7880
fax: 313-585-7884

CUBITAL LTD.
13 Hasadna St.
P.O. Box 2375
Industrial Zone North
Raanana 43650 Israel
972-52-919476
fax: 972-52-919937

Cubital was founded in 1987 as a spin-off of Scitex Corporation Ltd., an Israeli prepress electronic publishing firm. Currently, Cubital is a joint venture, owned by Scitex, Schneider Optik of Germany, Clal Electronics Industries Ltd. of Israel, and Maho AG of Germany.

Scitex had sent Itzchak Pomerantz, now president of Cubital, to a trade show in 1985 to look for a product that did not exist, would be in heavy demand in the mechanical engineering field, and fit within Scitex's "portfolio" of technologies. He decided the world needed a 7-foot $300,000.00 machine that would turn CAD files into plastic models. Further market research showed that the industry considered such an idea to be science fiction, but everyone had precise specifications for that fictional system, he later recalled. Size, accuracy, material properties, human engineering aspects, and price-performance requirements were gathered, and Scitex then spent about $10 million on development.

The resulting machine was somewhat larger and more expensive than envisioned, and Scitex had to learn photochemistry. A patent cross-license agreement was signed with 3D Systems in 1988 to head off any legal problems.

In the United States, Cubital has operated largely as a service bureau with one of its machines in the Detroit area. Sales of actual machines, however, have begun.

Solider® 5600
Size: 13 feet 6 inches long, 5 feet 7 inches wide, 4 feet 10 inches high (See Figure 2-6)
Model Size: 20 x 14 x 20 inches
Accuracy: 0.1 percent, up to 0.02 inch
X–Y Resolution: Better than 0.004 inch

Minimum Feature Size: 0.015 inch
Price: $495,000.00, delivered and installed

Cubital's Solider uses a variation of stereolithography called Solid Ground Curing (SGC), which differs radically from the approach taken by 3D. Each slice is cured before the next one is laid down, eliminating shrinkage and warpage considerations. Each slice is also milled to the desired thickness before the next one is laid down. (The milling device also allows the machine to erase flawed slices.) Since voids are filled with wax (as explained below), there is no need to add support structures to the CAD file. The Cubital machine's most evident advantage appears, however, to be its model-making "envelope," in which relatively large parts or multiple small parts can be made at one time. (See Figures 2-7, 2-8, and 2-9 for the appearance of finished parts.)

On the other hand, the machine itself is large, complex, and expensive. SGC is a complicated process, involving ten steps for each slice.

1. A resin applicator covers the work area with a film of photoreactive liquid polymer resin.
2. A negative image of the slice is printed on a flat glass plate, much as a laser printer will print an image on a sheet of paper. The image on the glass forms an "optical mask."
3. The optical mask is placed above the work area under a high-powered UV lamp.
4. A shutter opens for a few moments. The exposed resin is flooded with enough light not only to polymerize it, but also to cure it. Masked areas remain liquid.
5. The optical mask is wiped clean.
6. Unused (liquid) resin is vacuumed out of the work area.
7. A film of melted wax is spread over the work, replacing the liquid resin that was just removed and filling any cavities.
8. A chilled plate is pressed down on the wax to solidify it.
9. A milling disk flattens the layer and trims it to the specified height.
10. The model is lowered one slice-height, and the process begins again.

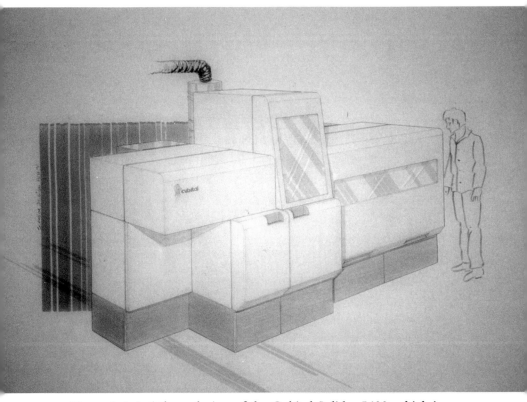

Figure 2-6. Artist's rendering of the Cubital Solider 5600, which is more than 13 feet long.

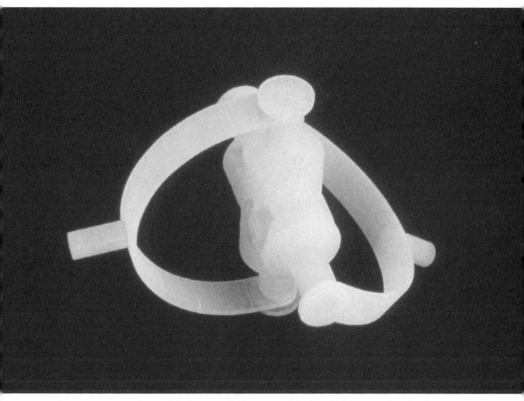

Figure 2-7. Universal joint made in a Cubital Solider 5600, which was functional when removed from the machine.

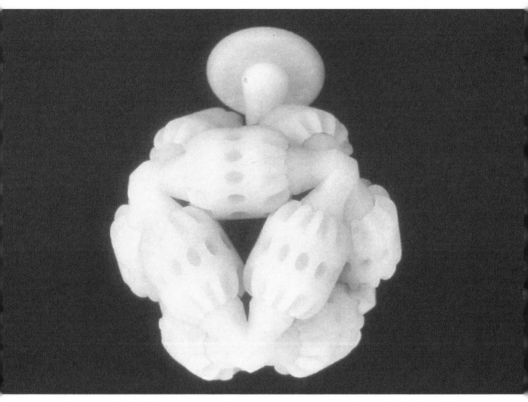

Figure 2-8. Multi-gear assembly made in one piece in a Cubital Solider 5600 model-making machine. The eight-gear device functioned when removed from the machine.

Figure 2-9. Geneva gear transmission assembly made in one piece in a Cubital Solider 5600, which functioned when removed from the model-making machine.

The Solider can do about 60 to 100 slices per hour. The end result is a solid block of wax containing the stereolithography model. The wax can be melted or washed away, or the model can be left in the block for machining or shipping or to maintain confidentiality.

Materials

The Cubital process involves three "consumables": resin, wax, and toner. Resin for the Solider 5600 is available from Cubital and from DSM Desotek. Details are covered in the Resin Vendors section later in this chapter.

The resin (called "Solimer™") is, of course, the photoreactive polymer from which the parts are created. The wax (called "Soliwax™") is the disposable material that supports the overhangs and voids of each layer. The toner (called "Solitone™") is used to create a mask image on a glass plate, blocking the UV light. It is wiped off the glass for reuse after each layer.

The wax is a nontoxic, nonhazardous, water-soluble variety customized for use in the Solider. The shelf life is said to be unlimited if stored properly — no exposure to water or to temperatures above 90°C. Its characteristics are as follows:

Softening Point (B&R): 65°C
Hardness Penetration: 7–9 Dmm
Density: 1.2 kg/m³
Viscosity at 67°C: 1500 mPa-s
Price: $4.20 per pound

The toner is a solid black powder that is 10–20 microns in particle size, apparently similar to that used in laser printers or photocopiers. The toner is recycled within the imaging unit of the Solider, and overall cost is reported to be negligible.

Software

The Solider comes with a Digital Equipment Corp. DECstation

5000/200 running Motif-based proprietary slicing software under a version of Unix. (See Figure 2-10.) Input is in the .STL format, which the software converts to Cubital's own format, called CFL (Cubital Facet List). CFL differs from .STL in that it is based on polyhedrons instead of triangles, reducing storage requirements. Negative values for "normals" indicate holes. The software can spot and cure small defects in the .STL input file. The software also has certain basic editing features, such as for cutting up large parts or adding text or logos to the part. Slicing is done in real time, rather than in advance, and the operator has the option of viewing individual slices on-screen.

Customer Reactions

Systems administrator for a maker of pumps on the Gulf Coast

After we started using rapid prototyping 18 months ago we ran into many problems (with service bureaus) we have had to overcome because our CAD system did not have .STL output. But, we have worked out the process with Cubital to the point where we can send them anything. The main reason is that the .STL converter that Cubital has is a much better piece of software — it will fix some of the problems that we have had. If it finds that two surfaces were joined in Boolean, and both are curved, Cubital's universal file translator will notice that they can intersect and will trim them.

We like the polymer that Cubital uses. It machines a little better (then 3D's) if we have to do any taps. We have even dropped a couple, and they have survived, whereas we have not dropped any 3D pieces, but I assume they would probably shatter.

The cost of prototype parts in investment wax is too high at this point for us to go into full tooling in investment casting — we have to have multiple investment casting models, so we can make 200 castings at a time. What rapid prototyping gives us is a quick way to manufacture a prototype pump. We have been going from a solid model to investment casting into a prototype pump for testing, but, for full production, the expense is too high. But, it cuts lead time on trying to cut a piece out of

Figure 2-10. The workstation of a Cubital Solider 5600 (a DECstation 5000/200) showing its graphical interface.

solid steel as opposed to getting a prototype made and having it cast in a matter of a few weeks. We have found casting vendors that can burn Cubital polymer models (out of investment casting molds). It's a matter of temperature and time.

We have taken the polymer Cubital parts to make working parts to put in pumps for tests. We burned a couple up, but we did put them in and ran them and learned enough to know what the output would be.

Engineer at a Detroit car company

I have noticed that people begin to depend on rapid prototyping after using it once.

We are in the process of buying a Cubital machine. We tried out all the different processes and did a decision matrix with a whole page of criteria weighted by importance. For our purposes, Cubital and Helisys were the top runners, with Cubital a bit ahead. None of the processes were as good as we would like in terms of accuracy — we would like 3–4 thousandths so we could use them as casting patterns, but nobody was in that range. Helisys was the most accurate, since there was no phase change or shrinkage on their part. But, there are many uses for rapid prototyping, and 90 percent of those applications can be adequately served given the current accuracy.

We prefer Cubital parts (over 3D's parts). In the beginning, it was due to the resins — the early resins were very brittle, but Cubital's was tougher. Now it's about equal, but you don't have the issue of supports in the Cubital machine. We do parts with internal cavities, and it's a pain to clean the supports out of them.

Otherwise the Cubital machine is (proving to be) horribly expensive. We are working on a facility to put the machine into. We don't want the odor (of the resin) to get out, so we have negative pressure in the room. But, when you run the machine, it sucks a lot of air out of the room, since it vacuums the unused resin and the milled chips in each layer. We have to heat or cool all that incoming air. The air compressor runs all the time and is noisy. We will have a separate control room for the operator with a plate of glass between the operator and the machine.

We are also concerned about accidents, in case a resin drum leaks over the weekend, since we do not want it to go into the sanitary sewer. So we pitched the floor to contain a certain volume of liquid, without being a barrier to pedestrians.

The machine does not use standard voltages, and we had to supply a transformer. The machine requires 10 bars of pressure, higher than the shop floor, so we needed a separate air compressor. And there will be a third room for the dewaxing machine.

The cost of the facility is expected to be $200,000.00

But, as long as we can keep the machine busy, it won't be any more expensive than any other method, since you can do more parts at a time.

Incidentally, a Cubital build session is called a show. Each part is called an actor. You may have to dedicate a show to a large actor and pack the smaller ones in around it. A small actor might be added to an existing show. In fact, you might be able to add it in on the top while the session is in progress.

Part size has and has not been an issue. At every meeting we went to to get the project approved, management asked how large a part it can build, so it is a concern from management's standpoint. But, you can put dowels in the CAD model and assemble the subsections later. Even that is not required very often.

Prototyping specialist for maker of computer printers on the West Coast

We have used Cubital. Their parts would seem to be good for larger, more flexible items that don't need a lot of accuracy, like duct work or plenums. I have not been very impressed with their parts. We had them make some paper trays, and there was some warp in them. And their surface finish is pretty poor, so you can't cast off it very well.

Resin Vendors

Stereolithography resin is an evolving field. For instance, the vendors originally used a compound called N-vinyl pyrrolidone (NVP) as a diluent that gave the resin lower viscosity and promoted interlayer adhesion. (Is is also rendered 1-vinyl-2-pyrrolidinone, or N-vinyl-2-pyrrolidone.) However, NVP was found to be carcinogenic, and the vendors have been replacing it with other chemistries.

Simarily, there now appears to be a move away from the use of acrylates, which are a sensitizing irritant (i.e., repeated exposure increases the subject's reaction). Acrylates are also said to be behind some problems with shrinkage and distortion. So far, only Allied-Signal has a resin that is both non–NVP and nonacrylate.

The properties are listed substantially as given by the vendors, with the prices as of late 1992. E_c refers to the photosensitivity of the resin, and D_p the depth (in terms of a formula decided by 3D Systems) to which polymerization will occur.

ALLIED-SIGNAL INC.
A-C Performance Additives
P.O. Box 2332J
Morristown, NJ 07962-2332
201-455-3120
fax: 201-455-6154

Allied-Signal sells a photoreactive resin called EXactomer 2201, designed for use with the 3D SLA-190 and SLA-250 model-making machines. The resin is touted as being revolutionary in the field, containing neither NVP nor acrylates, suffering minimal swelling or distortion, and with a green strength about 80 percent of the cured strength. (The acrylates were replaced with vinyl ethers.) The parts are said to be tough, rigid, and opaque and can be machined and polished without cracking.

The resin is also touted as having a long (6-month) vat life and negligible reactive vapor content that could fog the optics of the model-making machine. The E_c value is higher (indicating lower photosensitivity) than other resins, requiring slower laser travel rate or a higher-power laser, but it also means that there is less diffusion of the laser beam and therefore more precise polymerization (said an Allied-Signal spokesman). The resin also depends on carbocationic polymerization instead of free-radical polymerization.

Allied-Signal suggests draining and cleaning the vat of the SLA machine before using its EXactomer and provides detailed instructions for doing this chore. Heat curing (1–2 hours at 80°C) is recommended except for parts with thin walls, where UV curing is recommended.

The single-gallon price is quite high, but the 5-gallon price is more competitive. The author has encountered users who refer to EXactomer as the "premium" resin on the market.

EXactomer 2201 Properties

Liquid

E_c: 27 mJ/cm² +/- 20%
D_p: 7
Flash Point: >140°C
Viscosity at 30°C: 205 cps
Density: 1.13 g/ml

Cured

Curl, NCF_6 (weave style): <3%
Modulus: 211 +/- 40 KSI
Tensile Strength at Break: 8 +/- 1 KSI
(MPa = KSI/0.145)
Elongation at break: 8 to 10%
Hardness (Shore D): 80

Prices:

1 gallon: $855.00
4-gallon case: $2,844.00
5-gallon drum: $3,375.00
(1 gallon = 9 pounds)

CIBA-GEIGY CORPORATION
Tooling Systems
4917 Dawn Avenue
East Lansing, MI 48823
517-351-5900

3D Systems is the exclusive distributor for Ciba–Geigy CIBATOOL® resins, which are designed for 3D's SLA machines. (Ciba–Geigy, remember, is a part owner of 3D Systems.) All six resins currently offered contain acrylates.

(3D Systems Inc.; 26081 Avenue Hall; Valencia, CA 91355; 805-295-5600; fax: 805-257-1200)

For the SLA-500, there are XB 5131 and XB 5154. XB 5131 contains NVP, while the more expensive XB 5154 does not. XB 5131 was the first resin available for the SLA-500. The multipurpose XB 5154 (released in the summer of 1992) is touted as offering greater accuracy, toughness, and throughput, with enough flexibility to let parts snap-fit together, yet remaining tough enough to be machined. Their properties are shown below. Note that, for the cured properties, the XB 5131 was cured for 60 minutes, and the XB 5154 was cured for 30 minutes.

CIBATOOL SL XB 5131

Liquid Resin

    Appearance: Transparent
    Density at 25°C: 1.14 g/cc
    Viscosity at 35°C: 1,000–2,000 cP

Cured Properties

    Tensile Strength: 8,700–11,600 psi
    Tensile Modulus: 435,000–580,000 psi
    Elongation at Break: 2–3 percent
    Impact Strength: 3 kJ/m^2
    Hardness, Shore D: 87–91
    Glass Transition: 150°C
    Price: $1,860.00 for 18 kg (4.2 gallons)

CIBATOOL SL XB 5154

Liquid Resin

    Appearance: Clear

Density at 25°C: 1.12 g/cc
Viscosity at 30°C: 1,600–2,400 cP
Viscosity at 35°C: 1,000–1,500 cP

Cured Properties

Tensile Strength: 5,000 psi
Tensile Modulus: 160,000–174,000 psi
    With Weave Hatching: 160,000 psi
Elongation at Break: 11–19 percent
    With Weave Hatching: ~10 percent
Impact Strength: 20–25 kJ/m^2
Hardness, Shore D: 78
Glass Transition: 83°C
Price: $2,350.00 for 18 kg (4.2 gallons)

For the SLA-250, 3D offers the XB 5134-1, XB 5149, and XB 5143. XB 5134-1 is an early resin known for its unforgiving parameters. XB 5149 is a reformulation offering greater ease of use and wider operating parameters to create the same quality parts. XB 5143 is touted as being twice as tough as XB 5149. XB 5143 has NVP, while the other two do not.

CIBATOOL SL XB 5134-1

Liquid Resin

Appearance: Slightly opaque
Density at 25°C: 1.14 g/cc
Viscosity at 25°C: 1,750–2,550 cP
Viscosity at 35°C: 1,050–1,450 cP

Cured Properties

Tensile Strength: 3,635–7,250 psi
Tensile Modulus: 145,000–203,000 psi
Elongation at Break: 7–12 percent
Impact Strength: 10–20 kJ/m^2

Hardness, Shore D: 78–83
Glass Transition: 40°–60°C
Price: $455.00 for 4 kg (0.92 gal.)

CIBATOOL SL XB 5134-1

Liquid Resin

Appearance: Clear
Density at 25°C: 1.12 g/cc
Viscosity at 30°C: 1,600–2,400 cP
Viscosity at 35°C: 1,000–1,500 cP

Cured Properties

Tensile Strength: 5,000 psi
Tensile Modulus: 160,000–174,000 psi
With Weave Hatching: 160,000 psi
Elongation at Break: 11–19 percent
With Weave Hatching: ~10 percent
Impact Strength: ~20–25kJ/m^2
Hardness, Shore D: 78
Glass Transition: 83°C
Price: $575.00 for 4 kg (0.92 gal.)

CIBATOOL SL XB 5143

Liquid Resin

Appearance: Clear
Density at 25°C: 1.12 g/cc
Viscosity at 30°C: 1,600–2,400 cP
Viscosity at 35°C: 1,000–1,500 cP

Cured Properties

Tensile Strength: 5,000 psi
Tensile Modulus: 101,500 psi
Elongation at Break: >15 percent

Impact Strength: ~40 kJ/m^2
Hardness, Shore D: 78–82
Glass Transition: 80°C
Price: $510.00 for 4 kg (0.92 gallons)

For the SLA-190, 3D offers the XB 5139, whose low viscosity means the resin can settle in a timely fashion after the elevator lowers the part, without the use of wiper blades. Since it is tuned for the helium cadmium laser, it could also be used in the SLA-250 but is used almost exclusively in the 190. It contains NVP.

CIBATOOL SL XB 5139

Liquid Resin

Appearance: Transparent
Density at 25°C: 1.14 g/cc
Viscosity at 35°C: 300–600 cP

Cured Properties

Tensile Strength: 9,425–11,600 psi
Tensile Modulus: 435,000–507,000 psi
Elongation at Break: 2.5–3.5 percent
Impact Strength: 5–10 kJ/m^2
Hardness, Shore D: 85–90
Glass Transition: 100–120°C
Price: $575.00 for 4 kg (0.92 gallons)

CUBITAL AMERICA INC.

1307F Allen Road
Troy, MI 48083
313-585-7880
fax: 313-585-7884

Table 2-1. Characteristics of Solimer Resins

	Type G	Type F
Liquid State		
Appearance	transparent viscous	liquid
Density at 25°C	1,100 kg/m³	1,100 kg/m³
Viscosity at 35°C	1,600 mPa–s	1,600 mPa–s
Cured State		
Glass Transition	70°C	41°C
Tensile Strength	35 MPa	13 MPa
Elongation	16 percent	55 percent
Secant Modulus (2.5 percent strain)	880 MPa	230 MPa
Price [Free on Board (FOB) England]	$270/gallon	$270/gallon

Cubital's Solimer resins (see Table 2-1) are specially made for Cubital by Coates Brothers of the United Kingdom. The resins are available only from Cubital and work only in Cubital's Solider 5600. They have an acrylate base but no NVP. There are two Solimer varieties: G (for general purpose) and F (for flexible).

DSM DESOTECH INC.
1122 St. Charles St.
Elgin, IL 60120
708-697-0400
fax: 708-695-1748

Desotech sells three stereolithography resins, the DeSolite® SLR® 805 and 806 and the DeSolite 4112-143-1. The first two are designed for the 3D Systems SLA-190 and SLA-250 model-making machines. The third is intended for the Cubital Solider 5600. (Desotech is apparently the only vendor besides Cubital selling resin for the Solider.)

The 805 resin is touted as having low viscosity for easy draining and cleanup and faster elevator travel; improved durability; and can be used for investment casting. The 806 resin is touted as having a low viscosity and a high strength modulus. Both have acrylates but no NVP.

The 4112-143-1 resin is touted as being tough, with a fast cure rate. It contains both NVP and acrylates.

DeSolite SLR 805 Properties

Liquid Resin, at 25°C

> Density: 1.07 g/cc
> Viscosity: 200–400 cps

Green Strength

> Tensile Strength: 1,300 psi
> Secant Modulus: 19,000 psi
> Elongation: 22 percent

UV-Cured Strength

> Tensile Strength: 3,500 psi
> Secant Modulus: 78,000 psi
> Elongation: 10 percent

DeSolite SLR 806 Properties

Liquid Resin, at 25°C

> Density: 1.07 g/cc
> Viscosity: 200–400 cps

Green Strength

> Tensile Strength: 2,500 psi
> Secant Modulus: 53,000 psi
> Elongation: 10 percent

UV-Cured Strength

Tensile Strength: 9,000 psi

Secant Modulus: 162,000 psi

Elongation: 7 percent

Prices for either:

$352.00 for 4 kg

$1,376.00 for 16 kg

$2,688.00 for 32 kg

$3,360.00 for 40 kg

(Forty kilograms is recommended for filling an SLA-250.)

DeSolite 4112-143-1 (for Cubital Solider 5600)

Liquid Properties

Density at 23°C: 1,120 kg/m^3

Viscosity at 25°C: 5,100 mPa-s

Cured Resin

Glass Transition Tan Delta Peak: 100°C

Secant Modulus at 2.5 Percent Strain: 1,000 MPa

Tensile Strength: 36 MPa

Elongation: 18 percent

Shrinkage on Cure: 7 percent

Water Sensitivity After 24 Hours (250 μm films): 5.5 percent weight change

Degree of Cure (UV Dose at 90 Percent Ultimate Secant Modulus): 0.15 j/cm^2

Prices:

1 to 5 30-gallon drums

$3,852.00 per drum

6 to 10 30-gallon drums

$3,658.80 per drum

11 to 20 30-gallon drums

$3,476.40 per drum

5-gallon pail (18 kg net)

$643.86 per pail

E.I. DU PONT DE NEMOURS AND CO.

SOMOS Solid Imaging Materials Group
Two Penn's Way
New Castle, DE 19720
302-328-5435
fax: 302-328-5693

Dupont had been an early developer of a stereolithography model-making machine (called SOMOS, for solid object modeling system) but subsequently decided to get out of the model-making hardware business — but has remained active as a resin supplier. The chemical giant at this writing has two lines of photoreactive polymer resins, the SOMOS 2100/2110 line and the SOMOS 3100/3110 line.

The 2100/2110 resin is designed for the fabrication of flexible opaque parts, and it is touted as offering "wide process control, smooth surfaces, low shrinkage and curl, and high flexibility." The 2100/2110 resin is intended to be cured with heat. The 3100/3110 resin is designed for the fabrication of tough, nonbrittle transparent parts and is touted as being "highly transparent, polishable to an optical finish, easily cleaned, with high 'green strength.'" The 3100/3110 resin is intended to be cured with UV fluorescent light.

The 2100 and 3100 resins are optimized for use with argon ion lasers, such as used in the 3D Systems SLA-500, the EOS Stereos, and the Tejin Seiki Soliform systems. The 2110 and 3110 resins are optimized for use with helium cadmium lasers, such as are used in the 3D SLA-250. (The specification sheets, however, indicate that either resin can be used with either laser.)

All four resins are touted as being tough, nonbrittle, machinable, low-odor, and non–NVP.

2100/2110 Properties

Uncured

Appearance: milky white opaque liquid

Viscosity: 3420–4090 cP at 30°C

Density: 1.16 g/cm³ at 25°C

Linear Shrinkage: 0.5 percent

E_c: 3.5 mJ/cm² (2100)

    3.48 mJ/cm² (2110)

D_p: 7.2 mil (2100)

    4.65 mil (2110)

"Green" Properties (UV Laser-Cured, Typical)

Tensile Strength: 1.4 MPa

Elongation at Break: 12 percent

0.2 Percent Offset Yield: 0.47 MPa

Secant Modulus at 1 Percent Strain: 16 MPa

Yield Strength at 5 Percent Strain: 0.49 MPa

Hardness (Shore D): 32

Density: 1.184 gm/cm³

Heat-Cured Properties (Typical)

(Standard heat postcuring is 15 minutes at 168°C.)

Tensile Strength: 7.14 MPa

Elongation at Break: 46 percent

0.2 Percent Offset Yield: 0.57 MPa

Secant Modulus at 1 Percent Strain: 37 MPa

Yield Strength at 5 Percent Strain: 0.64 MPa

Hardness, Shore D: 41

Density: 1.195 gm/cm³

3100/3110 Properties

Uncured

>   Appearance: Transparent liquid
>   Viscosity: 970–1000 cP at 30°C
>   Density: 1.13 g/cm³ at 25°C
>   Linear Shrinkage: 0.7 percent
> E_c: 3.9 mJ/cm² (3100)
>   2.47 mJ/cm² (3110)
> D_p: 7.4 mil (3100)
>   4.98 mil (3110)

"Green" Properties (UV Laser-Cured, Typical)

>   Tensile Strength: 16 MPa
>   Elongation at Break: 16 percent
>   0.2 Percent Offset Yield: 6.9 MPa
>   Secant Modulus at 1 Percent Strain: 460 MPa
>   Yield Strength at 5 Percent Strain: 10 MPa
>   Hardness, Shore D: 77
>   Density: 1.201 gm/cm³

UV-Cured Properties (Typical)

>   Tensile Strength: 21 MPa
>   Elongation at Break: 9.2 percent
>   0.2 Percent Offset Yield: 13 MPa
>   Secant Modulus at 1 Percent Strain: 810 MPa
>   Yield Strength at 5 Percent Strain: 20 MPa
>   Hardness, Shore D: 80
>   Density: 1.205 gm/cm³

The base price for any of the SOMOS products is $550.00 for 4 kilograms or $2,700.00 for 20 kilograms. Further volume discounts are available.

LOCTITE® CORPORATION

705 North Mountain Road
Newington, CT 06111
203-278-1280
fax: 203-280-3558

Loctite is best known as the maker of SuperGlue, although it also makes various industrial adhesives and related products as well. Loctite offers two stereolithography photoreactive resins, called 8100 and 8101.

The 8100 resin is described as a general-purpose resin with high stiffness, designed for use on the 3D SLA-250. The newer 8101 resin is described as being more flexible and also designed for use in the SLA-250. The 8101 resin is also described as being free of NVP.

A Loctite spokesman said the firm plans to come out with a new line of resins in 1993 that will, among other things, replace the acrylates in the 8100 and 8101 with norbornene thiols, to enhance accuracy, strength, and flexibility and to reduce toxicity. See Tables 2-2 and 2-3 for the properties of cured Loctite 8100 and 8101 resin, respectively.

Table 2-2. Properties of Cured Loctite 8100 Resin

	Laser Cured	**Post Cured**	**Thin Film**
Tensile Strength	2500 psi	4700 psi	6300 psi
Elongation	21 percent	11 percent	6.7 percent
Modulus psi	41,000	150,000	227,000
Hardness, Shore D	50–55	70–75	80
Extractables	34 percent	6.5 percent	6.5 percent
Price per Gallon	$362.00		

8100 Properties

Uncured

>   Appearance: clear, free-flowing liquid
>   Specific Gravity 25°C: 1.12
>   Viscosity at 25°C: 2300 mPa–s
>   Flashpoint (TCC): >200°F
>   Shrinkage: 6.5 percent
>   Shelf Life: 1 year
> D_p: 5.62 mils
> E_c: 6.53 mJ/cm^2

8101 Properties

Uncured

>   Appearance: clear, free-flowing liquid
>   Specific Gravity 25°C: 1.09
>   Viscosity at 25°C: 2000 mPa–s
>   Flashpoint (TCC): >200°F
>   Shrinkage: 4.8 percent
>   Shelf Life: 1 year
> D_p: 5.9 mils
> E_c: 4.58 mJ/cm^2

Loctite also sells instant adhesives (to bond pieces into larger models), mold-making silicones, and hand cleaners.

Table 2-3. Properties of Cured Loctite 8101 Resin

	Thin Film	**SLA Tensile Bar**
Tensile Strength	3400 psi	2500 psi
Elongation	26 percent	20 percent
Modulus psi	142,000	106,000
Stress at Yield	3400 psi	2100 psi (extrinsic)
Strain at Yield	6 psi	2.5 psi
Hardness, Shore D	78	—
Extractables	2.8 percent	—
Price	(not released)	

Selective Laser Sintering 3

"Sinter" means to weld (or form into a homogenous mass) without melting and is usually used to refer to metallic powder, the individual particles welding to each other without the entire mass becoming molten.

Thus, from the name "selective laser sintering" you have probably already been able to envision the resulting model-making process: you deposit a layer of powder in a chamber that is heated nearly to the powder's melting point. You sweep a laser across it to form a slice of the object that you are building, just as is done in stereolithography, except that the laser has to be somewhat stronger. The particles hit by the laser are raised to their sintering point and bond to the particles around them. The rest of the powder is unaffected and can offer support for overhangs, etc. Further layers are deposited and sintered, and, when the process is finished, the unused powder can be poured out.

The advantage is that you can, in theory, use just about any material — functional parts could be made from metal. It could lead to manufacturing on demand — shipping and distribution could be obsolete concepts. It could be the next industrial revolution.

As we will see, however, things are not to that point yet. How soon they will be, if they ever can, remains a mystery.

The selective laser sintering (SLS™) process came to inventor Carl Deckard in a flash of inspiration. Inspiration, as Thomas Edison once pointed out, however, is only one percent of the process. The rest is perspiration.

"As far back as I can remember, I wanted to be an inventor or a scientist," Deckard said in an interview. "I'd been working on various inventions as far back as elementary school, with varying degrees of seriousness, such as an internal combustion engine with fewer parts or a more efficient way to build houses. But one of the ones I'd worked on all the way through undergraduate school concerned a way to make three-dimensional objects directly from a computer model with one unified step. I thought the problem through a couple of years before figuring out what approach to take. Then it took some time to figure out how to implement the idea. It was purely a mental construction — I did no experiments or even research, and I didn't even know what physics I wanted to use," he said.

About the time Deckard had thought it through, in 1986 he was also in engineering graduate school at the University of Texas at Austin and realized his idea might make a good graduate research project. He explained it to his advisor, Dr. Joe Beaman, who got funding for Deckard's research.

Another graduate student helped him build the first SLS machine in 88 days. (They called it Bambi after abandoning an earlier, overambitious design, dubbed Godzilla.)

"It looked sort of like a high-tech junk yard," recalls Peter Lewis, Austin resident and computer columnist for the *New York Times*, who visited Deckard's lab. "There were some old-fashioned computers and some jury-rigged laser system. Because the medium was black metallic powder everything was coated with black dust. It was a very humble looking incubator."

Initially rebuffed by investors, Deckard then had his encounter with Paul McClure, an engineering consultant who had heard about Deckard's invention through the university's patent counsel.

"I went over and met the inventor and saw a vision of the next Xerox — the three-D Xerox of the future — right there in Deckard's little laboratory," recalled McClure of that meeting in late 1986. "We decided to launch a firm right there."

He set up DTM (the initials mean Desktop Manufacturing) using a $50,000 grant from the National Science Foundation's Small Business Innovation Research Program. Then (in December 1987), he arranged for the worldwide exclusive licensing of the UT-owned patent on selective laser sintering to DTM in exchange for future royalties and (in a fairly unique arrangement) a part ownership of DTM.

(Incidentally, patent licenses issued by the University of Texas generally involve a nominal up-front payment and a royalty of about three percent on drugs — which have a high development costs — and five to six percent on other inventions. With DTM, UT's board of regents accepted stock instead of a lump sum payment and a lower than average royalty of four percent — to be split with Deckard — in recognition of the stock's possible value. UT, meanwhile, makes about a million dollars a year on patent licenses, but most of it is eaten up with lawyers' fees. It is said that the only university in recent memory to make a killing off patent licensing was the University of Florida, alma mater of Gatorade.)

DTM Corp.
1611 Headway Circle, Building 2
Austin, TX 78754
512-339-2922
fax: 512-339-0634

DTM now employs about 100 people in northeast Austin (including McClure as a director, plus Deckard and Beaman in various capacities). Intrigued by the potential new use of plastic that DTM represents, BFGoodrich made major investments in the startup firm and now owns more than half of it. After producing prototypes using a machine called the SLS Model 125 at DTM's headquarters in Austin and at a BFGoodrich facility near Cleveland, DTM began offering its first commercial machine in late 1992, the Sinterstation™ 2000.

Sinterstation 2000 (See Figure 3-1.)
Size: 115 inches wide x 56 inches deep x 75 inches high, 4500 pounds
Laser: 50-watt, CO_2
Spot size: 0.015 inch

Figure 3-1. DTM Corp's Sinterstation 2000, almost 10 feet
long, which can make parts in wax, plastic, and nylon.

Tolerances, inch: +/- 0.010 initially, 0.005 second pass
Model size: cylinder 12 inches in diameter, 15 inches high
Nitrogen supply: 1.5 cf/min, 50 psi minimum
Speed: 0.5 to 1 inch per hour
Power: 208 or 240 VAC, 70 amps
Price:
  $289,000.00
  $10,000.00 Breakout Unit
  $10,000.00 polycarbonate initiation
  $60,000.00 nylon initiation
  $80,000.00 casting wax initiation
Yearly Maintenance:
  $85,000.00 one material
  $90,000.00 two materials
  $95,000.00 three materials

The Sinterstation uses a carbon dioxide laser to build parts, working downward into a cylinder. The piston that forms the floor of the cylinder is lowered slightly as each layer of powder is added to the model and smoothed by a roller. Building takes place in an atmosphere of neutral nitrogen, and outside venting is required. (See Figures 3-2, 3-3, and 3-4 for the appearance of finished parts.)

The two tolerances shown indicate that the user can expect to get 10 thousandths of an inch accuracy on the first attempt. If that is not adequate, adjusting various operating parameters should result in five thousandths tolerance.

The Breakout Unit is a device that shakes or blows the unused powder from the model and breaks up any clods that have formed in the powder, allowing the powder to be used again in another model-building session.

The "initiation" fees for each material refers to operating software and operating training for the use of that material. (The higher cost for investment casting wax reportedly results from the considerable effort

Figure 3-2. A complex part rendered by a DTM Sinterstation in casting wax and then reproduced using production metal.

Figure 3-3. EDM (electronic discharge machining) electrodes produced in investment casting wax by a DTM Sinterstation and then cast in copper.

Figure 3-4. Miscellaneous objects produced by selective laser sintering on
a DTM Sinterstation.

DTM has put into that material.) The fee also includes 60 pounds of the material and a 6-month warranty.

The yearly maintenance contract includes ongoing maintenance, hotline support, recharging of the laser, and 250 pounds of each material.

Materials

Materials currently offered are investment casting wax, polycarbonate, and nylon (see Table 3-1). At this writing, the materials are available only from DTM. While DTM had planned to offer a form of hard ABS plastic, the idea had to be dropped — the plastic proved unexpectedly hard to optimize for, and there were toxicity concerns. Other engineering thermoplastics, however, are under development and may be out by the time this book reaches print.

DTM also hopes to come out with ceramic material (probably alumina) and low-temperature metal (probably copper) in 1993. The material will probably be mixed with polymer binders, and the resulting models will have to be postcured in a kiln to bake out the binder. Some shrinkage will result, but it is assumed that the shrinkage can be predicted with precision and adjusted for in the CAD design.

Table 3-1. Properties of Materials for Sintercasting

	Poly-carbonate	Nylon	Investment Casting Wax
Flex modulus	122,000 psi	160,000 psi	n/a*
Flex strength	4,800 psi	8,300 psi	n/a
Density	0.82 gm/cc	0.91 gm/cc	0.80 gm/cc
Particle size	95 percent <105 microns	95 percent <105 microns	95 percent <180 microns
Price	$65/pound	$65/pound	$65/pound

*n/a = not applicable

Software

The Sinterstation performs slicing and process control through a 486 PC running Unix and X-Windows. The PC is included in the price of the Sinterstation. The proprietary software will not perform CAD editing, but the user can reorient and view the object and get build status and time to completion estimates. Recent software enhancements allow the Sinterstation to run unattended.

Input is through .STL files. An IGES interface is also reported to be under development.

Customer Reactions

General manager of a rapid prototyping service bureau on the West Coast

We are a service bureau for rapid automated prototyping, and we are now (late 1992) the only service bureau with a DTM machine, and the only one that does both stereolithography and selective laser sintering. We had considered the possibility of getting another stereolithography machine, but, after looking at the potential technologies, we chose DTM because of its flexibility in materials. Investment casting is one of our main markets, and DTM's main product was investment casting patterns.

Because the DTM machine was in the beta stage, we had a big learning curve to deal with. There were a lot of changes both in the machine and in the software, but, at this point, we are making parts, and the machine is making money — but it still has a long way to go.

The tolerances are better with stereolithography.

With the DTM machine, sometimes we have had to make the part several times to get a good part. You have to make adjustments for the material you are working with, for the size of the part and for the geometry — for things like the surface area being scanned and how thin the walls are.

But we have been able to make usable parts in wax. We have been doing better in the last two months. We have gotten over some hurdles, but there are still more to go.

We use polycarbonate — the nylon has not worked well on our

machine. The material (of the finished models) does have some porosity, but we impregnate it with epoxy to seal it and strengthen it.

Porosity has not been a problem with the wax, which has a nearly 100 percent density.

We use stereolithography for design review, presentation models, and mold masters, and we use the DTM machine to make parts for functional testing. We have found it's better to take a stereolithography part, put a good finish on it, check the tolerances, and make molds from that. It's easier to get a good finish on a stereolithography part.

But we only use stereolithography on shapes that are easy to tool. Shapes that are not easy to tool are candidates for SLS wax, and we have done some incredibly complicated shapes in SLS. If it's complicated, and you want an investment casting pattern as the end result, it needs to be done with SLS.

If it's a simpler part, and they want multiple copes in the 10 to 100 range, we make a stereolithography part, pour an epoxy tool around it, put it in a wax injection machine, inject the wax into it, pop out that wax, set it up, and do another one, etc. and send the wax things to the foundry.

Manager of technical data processing for a maker of power hand tools on the East Coast

We use DTM's service bureau. We have used other forms of rapid automated prototyping, especially 3D Systems, and the reason we went to DTM is because of the material — we started with their polycarbonate material and then went to nylon. And we use wax models to make aluminum casts.

We do actual testing with the DTM prototypes — we assemble hand power tools and run them. The motor housing and the handle will be plastic, and the gear housing is aluminum. The rest is standard motors and gears. It has worked out well in that both the nylon and polycarbonate are strong enough that we can use the production fasteners (screws).

The polycarbonate, as it comes out of the machine, is not adequate for our purposes, but DTM does postprocessing — painting the part with viscous epoxy — that cures the porosity problem. Before the postprocessing, it had the feel of Styrofoam and was not suitable for our parts with thin walls (2-3 mm). With nylon that secondary operation is not necessary. The porosity of the nylon looks real good and seems to be 80–90 percent filled. So we have been using the nylon, which is good enough for snap-fit parts.

As for tolerances, the bearing bores have to be machined on the investment cast parts and sometimes the mating faces. Beyond that, tolerances have been adequate. Part sizes have not been a problem.

Previously we had (NC) machined prototypes. They can take a few weeks to a few months, depending on their complexity. Now we generally have turnaround times of a week to 10 days on plastic parts. Wax models take longer since they are sent to an outside investment casting shop directly from DTM. I have had 5-week turnaround times on investment cast parts, from sending in the diskette with .STL data to receiving the final part. It would have taken 8 weeks for a machined part. So the case of investment casting processing the new method is not a lot faster — but it is a lot cheaper, about 60 percent cheaper.

NC manager for a maker of computer printers on the West Coast

The DTM parts we have seen have been a little fuzzy, although we have not done any recent testing. Fine details are a little difficult to deal with, since there is a tendency toward rough surfaces. On a part with a 15 thousandths diameter hole in the surface, the hole would be all but closed up (by the roughness). I try to avoid that. But DTM probably has the best chance of long-term success, since they can use normal materials. So far I have not had the support of my customer group, saying these parts are good enough for what they are looking for. But I see a real strong market for what DTM has done in wax.

Engineer at a Detroit car company

DTM has made us polycarbonate and wax parts. The wax parts were fragile, but that is a function of the material. I was impressed with the toughness of the polycarbonate parts — they look fragile but you can throw them around.

Prototyping specialist for maker of computer printers on the West Coast

We started with DTM in the early phases of their development in about 1990. Our prototypes from them (at the time) were coming back inaccurate, and a few times we had to send them back and explain which axis was out of tolerance and give them feedback. But when we used them this year (1992) we were very pleased with their accuracy and resolution.

We still do postmachining on the bores and bosses, but that's true of all the rapid prototyping we do — holes or anything cylindrical have stairsteps in them, and, if there is a mating part that has to slide and fit, we machine that part afterwards.

We use DTM for large structural parts that need a lot of disassembly and reassembly, since they can handle being screwed together and unscrewed several times. And the parts are very stable — no postcuring problems or warpage.

But, for smaller parts, we would use 3D, since there is more definition on smaller features. DTM can't handle finer features, and, because of the particles it uses, the geometry is not crisp and corners are not sharp. 3D parts also have a better surface finish, and we would use them for anything we were going to cast from.

Fused Deposition Modeling 4

Fused deposition modeling (FDM™) involves putting down successive layers of material in such as way as to build up the model, new layers fusing to the previous layers before solidifying.

FDM is represented so far by Stratasys™ Inc. of Minneapolis, Minnesota, founded by married partners Scott and Lisa Crump.

STRATASYS INC.
14950 Martin Drive
Eden Prarie, MN 55344
612-937-3000
fax: 612-937-0070

Scott Crump is a mechanical engineer with specialization in materials and in heat-transfer. He and Lisa Crump had previously worked together in a start-up firm. They were both educated at Washington State University.

One day, Scott Crump was toying with some experimental low-temperature thermoplastic with their three-year-old daughter, rolling it into toy frogs and other shapes, and noticed that the layers would adhere. After she went to bed, he went out into his garage and started playing with the material seriously. After a week of experimenting, he saw that he could get the layers as thin as half a thousandth of an inch and decided to see if he could make three-dimensional models. At first he used an X–Y plotter, adding the Z movement manually. The sliced plots were created by the AutoCAD macro language.

The plotter went through seven iterations. A hopper feed was discarded for a filament spool. Water and freon cooling were discarded for air cooling.

Crump quit his job in 1988, and Stratasys was founded that year, partially funded by Battery Ventures of Boston. A machine was demonstrated in 1990, although the Z element was only three inches. Beta units were delivered in 1991 with a 12-inch Z element. In August 1992, Stratasys announced a development agreement with 3M.

In the autumn of 1992 the firm had 18 employees and had sold 18 units of its FDM machine, called the 3D-MODELER™.

3D-MODELER (See Figure 4-1)
Announced: 1990
Size: 30 x 36 x 68 inches, 250 pounds
Model Size: 12 x 12 x 12 inches
Resolution: +/- 0.005 inch
Wall thickness: 0.009 to 0.25 inch
Repeatability: +/- 0.001 inch
Speed: 15 inches of filament per second (see Figures 4-2 and 4-3)
Price: $182,000.00 ($162,000.00 without UNIX workstation)

The unit resembles an enclosed pen plotter, except that the plotter lays down heated plastic or wax instead of ink, building a model upward through successive laminations. A 0.05-inch filament of thermoplastic material is unwound from a spool and fed into a heated nozzle, at 1°F above the material's melting point. It solidifies as soon as it's extruded, adhering to adjacent material to form the model.

Stratasys claims an overall tolerance of plus or minus five thousandths on all three axes over the entire 12-inch-cubed working space. Repeatability, which measures how closely the machine can run the same tool part 100 times with the tool part remaining within tolerance and resolution, is put at plus or minus one thousandth.

Stratasys touts its modeler as being safe, fast, cheap, and flexible.

⋆ Safe, since there are no exotic chemicals or lasers in use and since the heat range (180 to 220°F) it uses is about that of a coffee maker.

Figure 4-1. The Stratasys Inc. 3D-MODELER FDM model-making machine, measuring 30 x 36 x 68 inches and weighing 250 pounds.

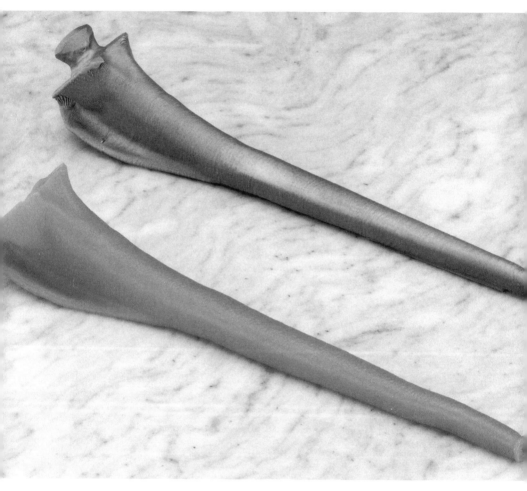

Figure 4-2. Hip replacement produced in Stratasys investment casting wax, bottom, and metal part cast directly from wax model, top. Creation time: 1 hour.

Figure 4-3. Airfoil produced in Stratasys machinable wax. Creation time: 5 hours 45 minutes. Resolution: 10 thousandths.

★ Fast, since there is no postcuring.

★ Cheap, since the unit is relatively inexpensive and since the materials average only about $5 per model. A golf club head takes about $9 worth of material and a half-mile spool would make about 20 heads. Also, no vents or other special facilities are required — you roll it into the shop and plug it in.

★ Flexible, since you are not limited to using photoactivated polymers or even the current generation of Stratasys materials.

The unit requires no venting and can be plugged into standard 110-volt outlets.

Materials

Stratasys offers three materials in a number of colors: machinable wax, plastic polymer, and casting wax.

The machinable wax is a wax-filled adhesive plastic material intended for conceptual modeling and spray metal molding.

★ Cost: $175.00 for a half-mile spool.

★ Color: blue or gray.

★ Properties: See Figures 4-5 and 4-6

The plastic filament (called PLASTIC200) can be used for sturdier models intended for conceptualization or form-fit-and-function testing.

★ Cost: $260.00 for a half-mile spool

★ Color: white

★ Properties: See Figures 4-7 and 4-8

The casting wax can be used to create conventional investment casting molds, where the model is melted during the process.

★ Cost: $175.00 for half-mile spool

★ Color: red

★ Properties: See Figures 4-9 and 4-10

Stratasys is the only source of these filaments.

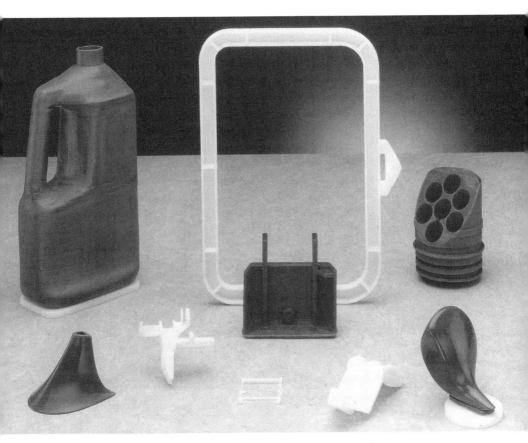

Figure 4-4. Miscellaneous objects produced by the Stratasys model making machine.

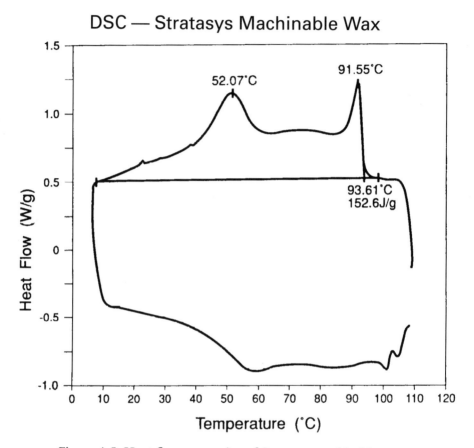

Figure 4-5. Heat flow properties of Stratasys machinable wax.

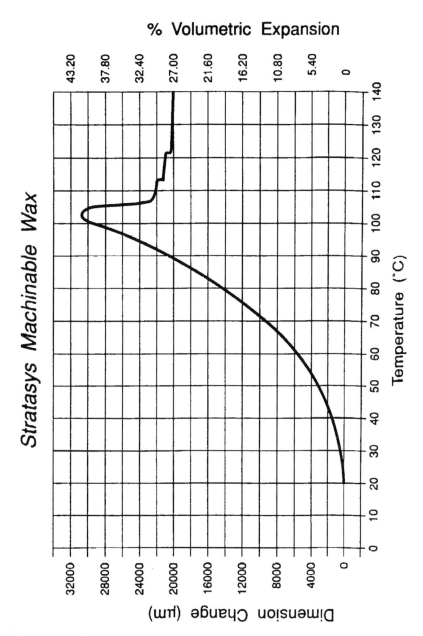

Figure 4-6. Volumetric expansion properties of Stratasys machinable wax.

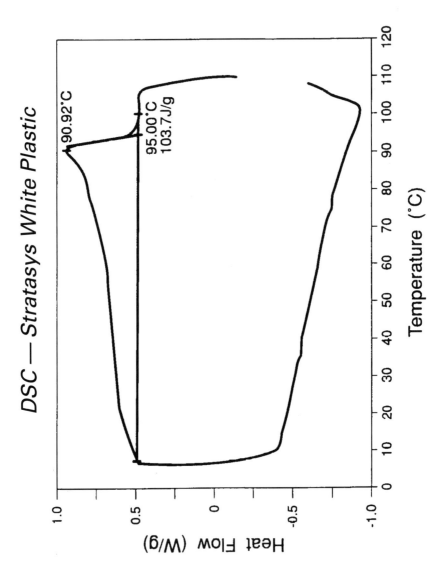

Figure 4-7. Heat flow properties of Stratasys plastic.

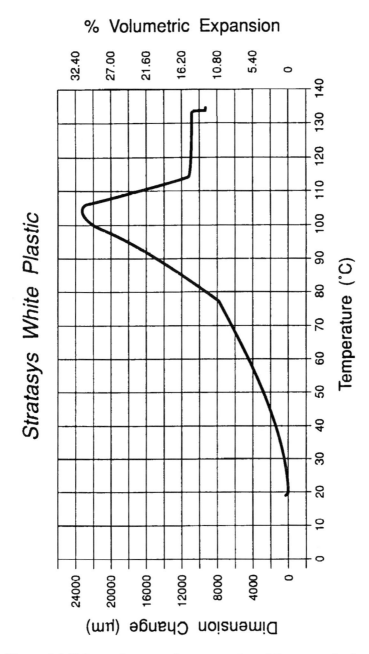

Figure 4-8. Volumetric expansion properties of Stratasys plastic.

FUSED DEPOSITION MODELING

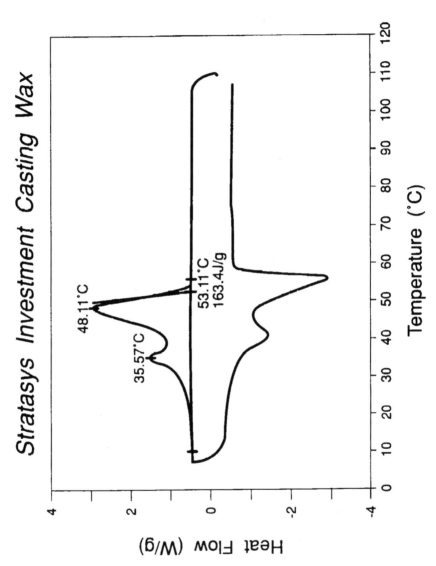

Figure 4-9. Heat flow properties of Stratasys investment casting wax.

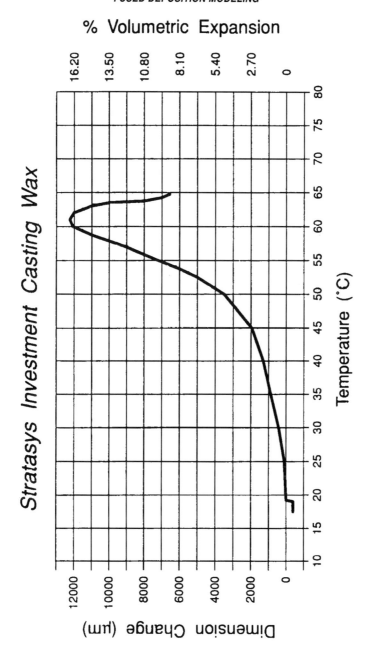

Figure 4-10. Volumetric expansion properties of Stratasys investment casting wax.

Software

The 3D MODELER is controlled by NC code through a standard serial port. The NC code can be input from any workstation that produces it, or the Stratasys workstation can generate the codes from IGES data or standard .STL files.

A user who already has a CAD system with NC code output can also use the NC code to drive the machine. NC commands are used in a reverse fashion — instead of cutting away material from the top down, material is added on from the bottom up.

IGES files imported into the Stratasys system can be surfaced, if needed, and supports added graphically. Through IDES, the unit can also import digitized data, such as produced by CAT or MRI scans, to define either slices or surfaces.

All geometric IGES entities are supported, while the drafting and working entities are not. Entities supported include the following:

100 Circular Arc

102 Composite Curve

106 Copious Data

110 Line

108 Plane

112 Parametric Spline Curve

114 Parametric Spline Curve

116 Point

118 Ruled Surface

120 Surface of Revolution

122 Tabulated Cylinder

124 Transformation Matrix

126 Rational B-Spline Curve

128 B-Spline Surface, Rational (NURBS)

142 Curve on a Parametric Surface

144 Trimmed Surface.

The Stratasys workstation software, called ProtoSlice™, includes a CAD package with a full NURBS-based surface modeler and can be used design a part from scratch.

Standard .STL files, in binary or ASCII format, can be used. The files are translated into NC code to drive the modeler.

Customer Reactions

President of a prototype maker on the West Coast

We chose Stratasys because it is so similar to using NC — instead of taking material off you're putting it on. Therefore, you can use the same software you used with NC.

We have gotten tolerances of plus or minus one thousandths, but it takes trails. On a small part you might make a part, measure it, scale it to the dimensions you want, and then get the second part to what (dimensions) you want.

You can make parts overnight — it really pays on complex parts. It might take a week to make a propeller (with NC) but two hours on the Stratasys machine.

The plastic parts are very durable. You can drop it or throw it against a wall. The wax parts are not as durable and take twice as long to make since the wax extrudes slower.

(There is also little maintenance, and scrapped parts can be ground up and sent back to be remade into filament, although you need to add virgin material so the filament won't be too brittle, he added.)

You do need to add supports, either manually or with software. On a letter T, the bar would sag, and you have to add a gusset. But when you are through you can just snap them off, like a trim tab on a model kit. With other modelers you have to machine them off.

If we were to sit here and refine the process with a certain material, we would make sure the machine has been set up and running for a while, that the temperature inside is consistent. If there is no fluctuation in temperature, you can control the model better. The material is being extruded at just above its solidification temperature, but it also has to melt the previous layer. If you get the feed rate and the temperature just right, you will get a nice solid part.

The cost of the material is the cheapest we looked at.

The clients will have misperceptions and might present us with a component that is not viable to do via rapid automated prototyping. Because the technology is so new, there is still some education needed.

While it can do intricate interiors and exteriors that would be a nightmare on a milling machine, a simple bowl would be better done on a milling machine.

The main disadvantage is the size of the envelope. A milling machine for the same price would have an envelop of 30 by 30 by 60 inches.

Owner of a metal fabricating firm on the West Coast

I was looking for a use for 4,000 square feet of office space we were hardly using since office automation had eliminated the need for clerks. Meanwhile, the electromechanical industry is very mature, and we were trying to get a larger piece of a shrinking pie. I wondered where the (economic) expansion in this country would take place and decided it would be in the engineering and product development areas. While a lot of production tends to go overseas, our strengths are in research and development and in prototyping. So I wondered how a job shop could take advantage of that, using our existing customer base. And I saw that rapid automated prototyping technology had come far enough for us to jump in.

We chose Stratasys by way of elimination. We felt 3D Systems was limited by its material — if it could not be made from polymer then it could not be used. And there were already a number of job shops in the area using 3D that were beating each other up, price-wise.

I felt the other technologies did not have the flexibility or were not ready.

With the Stratasys machine, we have made masters for investment casting parts, although nothing that was used for final production.

We have had no problems with precision. Investment casting parts are typically machined later — the casting process is not all that accurate, and they will routinely machine certain faces. We stake a tolerance of plus or minus five thousandths and are able to hold that.

(As for turnaround time) it can takes weeks with customers who give us a design on a soggy cocktail napkin. For those who give us a well-documented two-dimensional print that has to be entered into the CAD system, it can take 1 to 3 weeks. Since there is a lot of feedback that has to go on, we give them the three-dimensional plat for verification. The ultimate is a person who gives us a fully completed three-dimensional solid or wire frame surfaced CAD generated part, in IGES or .STL format. We would like to average a week to a week and a half turnaround time. But we can give overnight turnaround for an expedite fee.

Most of what we get is in CAD, and the major firms are mostly using three-dimensional CAD. But we still find little things that they can get by with on a drawing that we can't stand, like two lines on top of each other, or corners not closed, or leaving construction lines in.

The learning curve has been steep, but the learning has been at the workstation, not the modeling machine. Daily we find out new tricks — the wax does better this way, the plastic is better for this and that.

The plastic parts are better than those made by 3D and, depending on the configuration, can take various loads. But I would not want to use them for high pressure vessels for testing purposes.

Maintenance has so far (after four months) amounted to keeping the machine clean. There is no vibration, no venting, no fumes. I don't smell anything. It draws only seven amps.

We have had terrific reception from customers. One salesman was five for five. The customers are amazed when we promise them (a turnaround of) 2 weeks, and it ordinarily takes 16. We are trying to learn when to tell our customers that our technology is not suited for their needs.

All things being equal, if the parts were made on an NC machine, they would cost about the same as ours, but the NC machine can make it out of steel.

For plastic molding, you take our part and sink it into foam to where the parting line would be for a two-part mold, then take a paint sprayer that sprays metal particles 5 microns in diameter and build it (the particles) up over the part to an eighth of an inch, add cooling lines and backing, then do it to the other side, pull it apart, and you have a two-part mold. We don't do that in-house.

Director of customized implant services for a maker of biomedical implants and artificial joints in the Midwest.

We had benchmarked other prototyping systems and chose Stratasys for many reasons, including speed and the quality of the results. And there were no fumes — that was another point that attracted us.

The tolerances it gives are equivalent to those of the other technologies, but it's a great deal faster. And we can take the wax model generated by the Stratasys machine and take it to an investment casting house and have that same shape produced in metal.

We have also been able to use CAT scan or MRI data (to image the patient's bone structure on a CAD system), make a device to fit it, and download the file to the Stratasys machine.

The processing time (for model building) is typically less than four hours.

We went to rapid automated prototyping out of a general need to produce a prototype of a new device quickly, since it is easier to discuss it with a doctor if he or she has a physical part to look at.

For casting, you put the appropriate gates at their locations, and that's generally it. Machining is done on a part after it comes back from the vendor, usually to put in precision tapers so it can be locked into other pieces.

NC manager for a maker of computer printers on the West Coast

The Stratasys machine leaves a small seam at the point where each layer begins. The seam can be worked, and they have made large steps in improving the situation, but most of our parts are machine precision parts, and we can't afford to have a seam come through.

Lamination Methods 5

Lamination implies the laying down of layers of material at normal temperatures and gluing them together. If each layer can be shaped and placed precisely, an accurate model can be built.

Two firms are currently approaching the idea with two different methods. Helisys is gluing together layers of paper and foil to produce models. Soligen is gluing layers of powder to create mold shells — the model stage is skipped entirely or assumed to have already been passed. As this is written, only Helisys has sold any machines. (Landfoam Topographics of Needham, MA, has a patent on a lamination method that would allow selective coloring and variable slice thicknesses but has not attempted to bring the design to market.)

HELISYS INC.
2750 Oregon Court, Building M-10
Torrance, CA 90503
310-782-1949
fax: 310-782-8280

Michael Feygin always wanted to be an entrepreneur, but that was hard to do in his native Soviet Union. But at age 23 he managed to leave, thanks to the Carter Administration's pressure to allow Jewish emigration. After getting a master's degree in Illinois, he decided to launch his own business. Then, in 1984, he happened to glimpse a magazine headline announcing research into model-making with lasers. Musing about how that would be possible, he came up with the idea of "Laminated Objected Manufacturing®" (LOM®). Later, he actually read the article and found it was about a completely different technology; but Feygin approached the author with his LOM ideas and got an encouraging response.

Over the next 3 years, he got research and development grants from the Department of Energy, the State of Illinois, and the National Science Foundation, totaling about half a million dollars. Helisys was originally incorporated (as Hydronetics Inc., reflecting Feygin's activity as a fluid mechanics consultant) in 1985 in Illinois. The firm moved to the Los Angeles area in 1989 when Feygin's wife (a Minsk native) entered medical school. A California power ski firm was already using the name Hydronetics, so the name was changed to Helisys — a meaningless name that let Feygin keep his H logo.

In the autumn of 1992 the firm had 12 employees and had sold about 15 machines.

LOM-1015 (See Figure 5-1)
Announced: 1990
Size: 44 inches long x 40 inches wide x 45 inches high
Model Size: 13.5 inches long x 10 inches wide x 15 inches high
Resolution: +/- 0.010 inch overall
Laser: 25 watt CO_2
Laser Beam Diameter: 0.010 to 0.015 inch
Laser Speed: 15 inches per second
Power: 15 amps
Exhaust: outside venting
Price: $85,000.00

LOM-2030
Announced: 1992
Size: 81 inches long x 53 inches wide x 51 inches high
Model Size: 30 inches long x 20 inches wide x 20 inches high
Resolution: +/- 0.010 inch overall

Figure 5-1. The Helisys LOM-1015 model-making machine.

Laser: 50 watt CO_2
Laser Beam Diameter: 0.010 inch
Laser Speed: up to 15 inches per second
Power: 20 amps
Exhaust: outside venting
Price: $140,000.00

The LOM machines lay down, from a roll, a sheet of paper or plastic with a film of heat-activated glue on one side. After the material is laminated to the previous layer by a hot roller, a laser incises the outline of the slice. The unused material is left in place, automatically supporting any overhangs, although it may be diced with cross-hatches by the laser for easy removal. Then, the next layer is laid, laminated, and incised, etc.

By all accounts, the resulting models are fairly durable, appearing to have been carved from fine plywood. If unpainted, they appear to be coated with graph paper, the result of the cross-hatching the laser did on the top layer so subsequent layers would not adhere. (See Figures 5-2 through 5-5.)

Helisys touts its machine for accuracy, simplicity, and speed.

* Accuracy, since there is almost no shrinkage or warpage.
* Simplicity, since overhangs are not a problem, and there is no postcuring or exotic chemicals.
* Speed, since the LOM machines perform faster on larger parts, if only because they do not have to be done in sections.

The resulting models are also cheap, since they are made from paper. The LOM 2030 also has the largest working envelope of any rapid automated prototyping system on the market.

Materials

Helisys offers two materials, paper and polyester film, both coated on the back with a heat-activated polyethylene glue. The firm urges users to

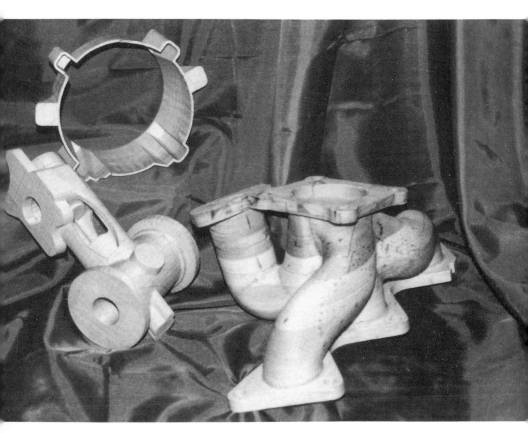

Figure 5-2. Helisys LOM models of varying complexity.

Figure 5-3. Helisys LOM models of varying size and complexity.

Figure 5-4. Crankshaft model made with the Helisys LOM machine.

Figure 5-5. (Right) LOM model of an electric box cover. (Top) Rubber mold of the model. (Left) Metalized epoxy mold. (Bottom) Aluminum casting.

use the paper, since it is much cheaper, and the resulting models serve most purposes perfectly well.

★ Paper: basically, butcher paper with a glue coating. Helisys sells it in rolls for $2 per pound but supplies customers with information on how to order it directly from paper companies, where it is said to be widely available.
★ Polyester film: sold by Helisys for $2 per square foot. Produces models with more flexibility than the paper versions.

The material used by the machine can vary from 2 to 20 thousandths of an inch in thickness.

Helisys is also reportedly working on a ceramic film that could be used to make production models directly.

Software

The LOM machines come with a 486-based PC running Microsoft Windows and the Helisys proprietary slicing software, called LOMSlice. The software does slicing only — some other package must be acquired for CAD work.

Input is in the form of .STL files.

Customer Reactions

Vice president of a Detroit prototype and small run plastics and casting supplier

Using Helisys, we have seen a 30 to 60 percent reduction in pattern building times. A typical run time (with the LOM machine) is 8 hours, that might take 4 weeks in a pattern shop. We still bill in hours, and it might take 40 hours to make the part, but with a machine, 40 hours means 2 days. To the clients, we are taking weeks out of a job. The clients are very intrigued by it when we start telling them about it, and they are familiar with conventional methods in wood or plastic.

The patterns are highly accurate. That was one reason we chose LOM, since we did not want to have to do a lot of rework on the models — we wanted to go straight off the LOM machine and into the model-making process.

We have gotten plus or minus five thousandths accuracy overall. If it needs to be finer, we can do machining. But clients want tighter and tighter tolerances all the time.

On certain types of geometries, like an exhaust manifold, we will do the inner core on the Helisys machine and hold tight tolerances. But we are also replicating the surface of a CAD file exactly, where a pattern maker working off a two-dimensional drawing would have to cut cross sections every few millimeters, and he would be interpreting what that would look like. And doing the inside, the air flow area, is critical. The rest of the design is just material thickness, and we are not concerned about what the outside looks like. So in this case we get a precision that's better than you would get in a pattern shop.

You also have to be literate in CAD. We get incomplete files or files where the surfaces aren't trimmed. But if you get an .STL file you can just load it into the machine.

There are a few things you have to learn about setting up the machine, but it's a short learning curve. All the models we have taken off the machine we have been able to use as patterns. There is no learning curve involved in getting accurate parts. We have not had to tweak the machine.

The LOM 2030 will be big enough for everything we do. We do a lot of automotive work and power train work, and even a power train could fit in that machine. Maybe not big diesel engines, but we have pattern makers who could fit the smaller sections together.

We have only used paper, but I can see how plastic could be an advantage. Paper is fine for our current purposes, but durable plastic might let you make a mold instead of a pattern and use it as a foundry tool.

Paper, of course, is only a fraction of the cost of polymers, but that was not a factor in our choice.

In general, there is a cost savings in using LOM over conventional methods, but it depends on how fast we have to expedite the job and how much CAD work there is. Well over 70 percent of our clients are using three-dimensional CAD, but not all are taking full advantage of it.

Account manager of a Detroit design and engineering firm

We were looking into stereolithography and came across the LOM process. We were looking for a process to build three-dimensional models from CAD data and verify a design. LOM seemed more economical, quicker, and involved less cost to develop the model process. It was about half the price of a stereolithography machine, the material is less expensive and nontoxic, and it is faster since the laser only needs to cut the perimeter (of a slice). Stereolithography machines have to cure the volume of a section and so spend a lot of time running across it.

The machine also comprises everyday technology. The laser is off the shelf. If there is something that breaks you can fix it fast. We have run the machine for 9 months with very few problems.

We have worked with customers to make molds and other parts from LOM models, not only to be used in tooling but also for presentations to the customers' customers. If they have a concept design for a part they want to sell, we will make an LOM model, in any scale, and they can make the presentation in three-dimensions.

Since then, we started doing design validation models, and other things such as tooling aids, duplication aids, foundry patterns, and models in silicon molds for cold-pour urethane.

Modeling time depends on the complexity of the design and the amount of CAD data available — it's different each time. If a customer comes to us with an .STL file, we can turn that around in one day. With a two-dimensional drawing, it will take more time. Most of the time is taken up at the CAD stage.

The last couple of programs were turned around in 5 to 6 days. One was a presentation part, with eight pieces. Another had a design prove-out that had three pieces, It took about 4 days including design work.

There is no postcuring process — the model is done when you're through. If we want to put it into the tooling process we may sand it for a better finish or paint it for a presentation.

The tolerances have been good. When we got involved, Helisys said it was plus or minus three thousandths. We tell our customers plus or minus five thousandths, and we have no problem meeting that. In the automotive field higher tolerances would be overkill anyway. Our (present LOM 1015) machine has a 10 by 15 by 16 inch working area, and the tolerances are for the whole box, so the tolerance is very good inch by inch.

We don't know how accurate we could be. We may be able to get plus or minus one thousandths on a small part.

You don't have to build supports, since the scrap material supports any overhangs. You can stop the building process to clear out any internal voids, or cross-hatch it until it comes out. For instance, if you were making a hollow ball, you would stop the process when it was still open at the top, remove the scrap, and finish it out.

We have been able to receive .STL files from every CAD system we have worked with, with no problems. If there was a glitch, it was usually caused by a hiccup when the file was written, and we ask for a new tape.

We don't see LOM as a tool for production at this point. It could be one, eventually, but the technology is not there. Most of the production molds we deal with are cut from aluminum or steel since they have to withstand the continuous injection pressure and temperature. Any (mold) material we could cast directly to the models would be too malleable to work on long-term production runs.

SOLIGEN INC.
19329 Bryant St.
Northridge, CA 91324
818-718-1221
fax: 818-718-0760

Soligen was founded by three former executives from 3D Systems

(Yehoram Uziel, Adam Cohen, and Chick Lewis) with venture capital backing, with the idea of automating yet another step in the industrial design process. The Soligen machine assumes that the design has been made; the patterns have been fabricated, tested, and approved; and it is now time to produce a casting mold. Instead of producing an object matching a CAD file, Soligen would produce a shell around a hollow void that would embody a mold for the part, with cores and gates fitted in. Molten metal can then be poured into the mold, creating the final part.

They call this approach Direct Shell Production Casting (DSPC). They count eight steps in a conventional investment casting process, which they hope to cut to two.

Conventional Process

1. Make dies for the part and its core.
2. Mold the cores.
3. Mold patterns on cores.
4. Connect the plumbing trees.
5. Dip in slurry.
6. Dry the shell.
7. Remove the wax.
8. Cast the metal.

DSPC Method

1. Print the shell and core.
2. Cast the metal.

Soligen hopes to cut lead times to 2 to 10 days, with only a few hours of labor between the completion of the CAD design to the pouring of metal, and, hopefully, functional parts can be had for the price previously paid for wax patterns. As this was written, Soligen had ten employees and was working on its first DSPC machines.

DSP-1

Announced: 1992
Model Size: initially 8 x 12 x 8 inches
planned 16 x 16 x 20 inches
Resolution: probably +/- 0.050 inch ("Equivalent to 3D Systems.")
Price: ("Equivalent to a small 3D Systems unit.")

Each slice of the shell is made by depositing a thin layer of alumina or some other ceramic powder and then applying the binder, using a process similar to ink-jet printing. The powder that receives the binder forms the outline of the shell at that layer. The process is repeated for each layer, the shell is heated to cure the binder, and then the unused powder is poured out. The shell can then be used as part of a conventional casting process. See Figures 5-6 and 5-7 for examples.

The shell-making process is licensed from two professors at the Massachusetts Institute of Technology.

Soligen touts DSPC for medical implants (often cast of exotic materials, with CAD-based modifications desirable), structural parts whose geometry makes them difficult to produce using conventional methods (such as gear housing, pump housings, gimbals for scanners, etc.), fast-turnaround molds for injection molding, and parts with complex internal passages (such as RF antennas and engine manifolds.)

Materials

The shells are made from alumina powder with a colloidal silica binder. Reportedly, the material is already widely used in the investment casting industry, and Lewis anticipates that customers will get it from suppliers rather than from Soligen. Lewis estimates the cost at about eight cents per cubic inch.

Software

Soligen is expected to include a software package called Layer with its

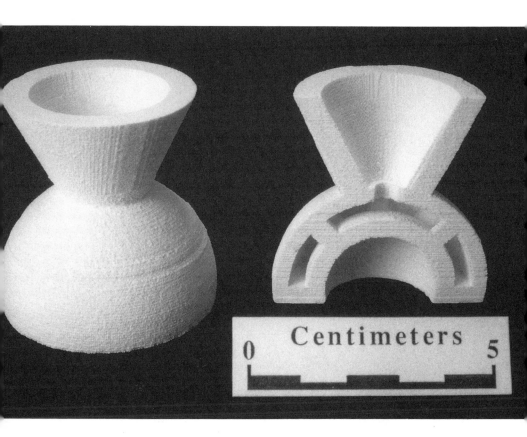

Figure 5-6. Soligen DSPC test mold.

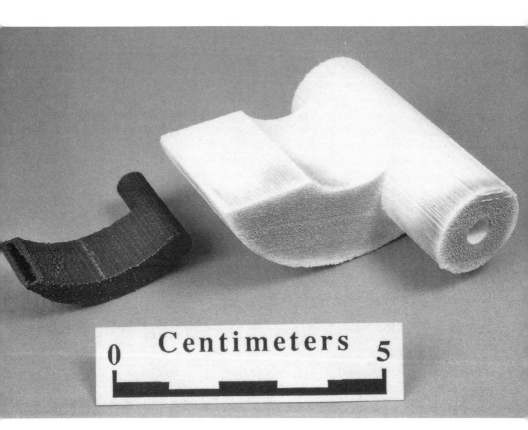

Figure 5-7. Soligen DSPC test parts.

machine, which will perform slicing and add gates and runners. It will accept .STL files as input.

Customer Reactions

(Soligen was building units for three "alpha" customers at the end of 1992. These customers are expected to become "development partners" of the DSPC technology.)

Scanners 6

Three-dimensional scanners are often used in conjunction with prototyping machines, either to check the output or to capture the design of parts for which no documentation exists. Two brands were encountered in use in modeling shops that used rapid automated prototyping — from Cyberware and from Laser Designs Inc. With its inclusion of color, the Cyberware machine would seem to be aimed slightly more toward animation and design than industrial use. (The scanner that comes with the EOS system is discussed with its model-maker in Chapter 2.)

CYBERWARE LABORATORY INC.

8 Harris Court
Monterey, CA 93940
408-373-1441
fax: 408-373-3582

The Cyberware system is broken into three mix-and-match components — the digitizer, the motion platform, and the software.

Digitizer

Cyberware's 3030 digitizer head is a (Class II) laser scanner that works with any of the four motion platforms described below. There are three variants: the 3030R which captures range information only (no color); the 3030RGB, which captures eight bits each of red, blue, and green, plus range; and HIREZ (which can be R or RGB) for smaller field, higher resolution scanning. The specifications are given in Table 6-1.

Table 6-1. Cyberware Digitizers

Field of View	3030R/3030RGB	HIREZ
x (or theta)	depends on platform travel typically 150 mm to 1 m, or 90-360°	
y at minimum z	260 mm	130 mm
y at maximum z	340 mm	170 mm
z	300 mm	150 mm
Resolution		
x (or theta)	depends on motion platform speed but typically 500 μmeter to 2 m	
y, μmeters	628	313
z, μmeters	100–400★	50 to 200★

★depends on surface quality

Motion Platforms

Cyberware offers four motion platforms — the desktop LN and CD units, the bench-size MS, and the person-sized PS.

The LN provides a linear scan path — the digitizer moves along a rail, scanning one side of a stationary object in less than 30 seconds. You can reposition the target and perform multiple scans to get a complete three-dimensional image. It can scan object as long as 50 cm with a typical minimum resolution of 0.5 mm and a maximum accuracy of +/- 0.1 mm. (The resolution can be controlled through the software.)

The CN model is a rotating platform placed in front of a stationary digitizer. Speed and accuracy are the same as the LN.

The MS platform is a bench with parallel one-meter rails on the top that can carrying a rotating platform past the stationary digitizer, thus offering both linear and cylindrical scan paths.

The PS platform is a 170-cm hexagonal rotating platform that a person can sit on and rotate in front of a stationary digitizer, which is generally positioned at the level of the subject's head and shoulders. (See Figure 6-1.)

Figure 6-1. The Cyberware PS scanning platform and (to the right of the subject's head) digitizer.

Software

Cyberware offers two software packages, named Echo™ and Plexus™. Echo lets the user view, scale, and edit scanned images and output them in various formats. Plexus lets the user combine multiple scanned images to create large, complex models.

The software is intended to run on a Silicon Graphics or Sun workstation, or a high-end PC. The PC version (see the price list below) does not include the Plexus software.

Echo outputs include NC tool paths, and optionally Autodesk, Parametric Technology, Wavefront Technologies, Alias Research, and Control Data CAD file formats. Plexus outputs include IGES and AutoCad file formats.

Prices:

Silicon Graphics versions

3030 R/I 3D Digitizer: $44,200.00
3030 RGB/I Color Digitizer: $53,200.00
3030 R/HIREZ/I Color Three-Dimensional Digitizer: $55,200.00

PC (DOS) versions

3030 R/D 3D Digitizer: $35,400.00
3030 R/HIREZ/D Color Three-Dimensional Digitizer: $38,200.00

Motion Platforms

PS: $10,000.00
MS: $22,600.00
LN: $7,200.00
CN: $7,200.00

LASER DESIGN INC.
9401 James Avenue South #162
Minneapolis, MN 55431
612-884-9648
fax: 612-884-9653

Laser Design offers four different scanner models for reverse engineering, mold-making, and quality assurance. Each is based on Class IIIb
lasers (eye protection recommended). The smallest model is a "retrofit"
for a vertical machine tool, while the others are free-standing bench-style
units.

Surveyor® Retrofit Model 100
Resolution: +/- 0.001
Average Maximum Speed: 75 points/second
Positioning: x,y,z, (rotation optional)
Price: $47,500.00

Surveyor Model 500 (See Figure 6-2)
Resolution: +/- 0.00125
Accuracy: +/- 0.002 (3-axis)
Envelope (inches): x=12, y=6, z=6
Average Maximum Speed: 80 points/second
Positioning: x,y,z, partial rotation optional
Price: $69,500.00

Surveyor Model 2000 (See Figures 6-3 and 6-4)
Resolution: +/- 0.0015
Accuracy: +/- 0.002 (3-axis)
Envelope (inches): x=12, y=18, z=12
Average Maximum Speed: 80 points/second
Positioning: x,y,z, part rotation optional
Price: $149,900.00

Surveyor Model 3000
Resolution: +/- 0.00125
Accuracy: +/- 0.002 (3-axis)
+/- 0.0035 (4-axis)
+/- 0.005 (5-axis)
Envelope (inches): x=15.7, y=23.5, z=11.8

Figure 6-2. Laser Design's Surveyor Model 500 scanner. (The device that appears to be a stool is actually the housing for the electronics.)

Figure 6-3. Laser Design's Surveyor Model 2000 scanner.

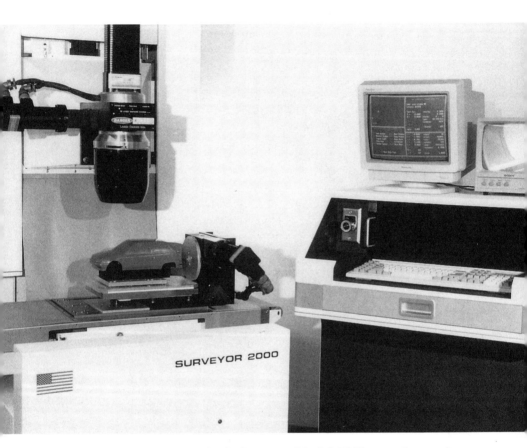

Figure 6-4. Laser Design's Surveyor Model 2000 scanning a clay car model mounted on an A-axis rotating bed.

Average Maximum Speed: 80 points/second
Positioning: x,y,z
4th axis (laser head) optional
4th axis (part rotation) optional
5th axis (laser head) optional
5th axis (part rotation) optional
Price: $220,000.00

Output from each system is in the form of IGES files. Laser Design optionally offers its DataSculpt data editing software for Silicon Graphics or high-end PCs, with NC and .STL file output.

Software 7

As stated throughout the book, most uses of rapid automated prototype depend on CAD, especially solid-modeling CAD. This book will not attempt to be a guidebook on CAD (a very large topic), but we will look into three CAD niches specific to rapid automated prototyping: .STL files, CAD programs that output .STL files, and structural support generating software for stereolithography machines (specifically Bridge-works.)

.STL Files

When a specification indicates that a model-making machine can accept .STL files, it is referring to a solid-model data representation method developed by 3D Systems and since widely adopted by other vendors. The name refers to the extension used for the data file, following the MS-DOS file naming practice of having an eight-letter name and a three-letter "file extension." CUBE.STL would be an .STL file named CUBE. STL, of course, is short for stereolithography.

An .STL file represents the surface of an object as an array of triangular facets. (Many CAD packages use facet geometry for screen rendering, making the use of facets compatible with most packages that offer surface or solid modeling.) Four data items (with three coordinate points each) are used to represent each facet — one item for each corner or "vertex" of the triangle and a fourth representing "facet normal."

Facet normal information and the vertex order are used to distinguish the model's outside from its inside. The normal vector points away from the surface of the object. The "Right Hand Rule" is also used to tell the inside from the outside — the vertices must be ordered so that as the fingers of the right hand move from the fist to the second to the third point, the thumb will represent the direction of the normal vector and will point to the outside.

The other rule of facet creation is the "vertex-to-vertex" rule — each adjoining triangle must share two points in common. The vertex of one triangle cannot be in the middle of the side of an adjoining triangle (as in Figure 7-1). Instead, they must share the same corner points (as in Figure 7-2).

The software can use any unit of measure for designating the vertices, but negative and zero vertices are not supported. (Zero values for individual coordinates are supported, however.) Every point on an edge must be embodied in a facet. Facets so small that they collapse into a line are said to cause no problems, but overlapping facets will cause stray lines in the model.

Obviously, flat surfaces with linear edges are easy to represent with triangular facets. Curved surfaces may require the use of tiny facets to render accurately the curves within the tolerances of the model-making machine. Tiny facets, of course, require more data, larger files, and more processing time.

There are two ways of representing data in an .STL file, ASCII and binary, which we will now examine.

ASCII Representation

When represented in ASCII, an .STL file can be comprehended by the human reader, but it takes up about five times more disk space than binary representation. (An ASCII example provided by 3D Systems, describing a simple rectangular box, takes up 3,310 bytes. The binary version takes up 684 bytes.) Therefore, ASCII versions are used mostly for test and demonstration purposes.

There are seven key words or phrases in an ASCII .STL file. They

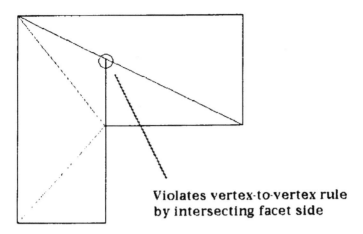

Violates vertex-to-vertex rule
by intersecting facet side

Figure 7-1. This part violates the vertex-to-vertex rule of .STL file representation since the vertex of one facet lies in the middle of the side of another facet.

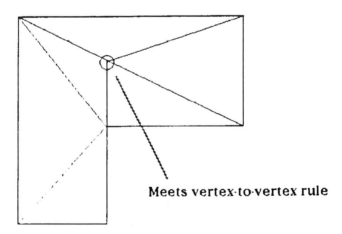

Meets vertex-to-vertex rule

Figure 7-2. The part now conforms to the vertex-to-vertex rule of .STL file representation as all the facets share two vertices.

must be separated by spaces (not tabs), and they must be written in lowercase:

* solid
* facet normal
* outer loop
* vertex
* endloop
* endfacet

* endsolid

Then, a specific order of data in the file must be maintained. An example follows.

```
solid [part name]
     facet normal 0.000000e+000 1.0000000e+000 2.634149e-009
          outer loop
               vertex 3.000000e+000 1.400000e+000 4.000000e+000
               vertex 4.000000e+000 1.400000e+000 4.000000e+000
               vertex 3.000000e+000 1.400000e+000 3.000000e+000
          endloop
     endfacet
```

The file will then go on to describe each facet with a "facet normal ... endfacet" loop. When the description is finished, the endsolid keyword appears.

Binary Representation

When examined (or "dumped"), the binary .STL file will look like a jumble of hexadecimal numbers, which is basically what it is. The coordinate points of the vertices are represented in IEEE floating point format.

Each file begins with an 80-byte space for a human-readable ASCII description of the file. There follow four bytes giving the number of facets in the object. Then, each facet is defined, with a four-byte floating point number for each coordinate of the normal and each vertex, followed by a two-byte "attribute" descriptor. (The attribute descriptor was left in for future use and is not actually used for anything. These two bytes are therefore left at zero.) The file is read until an end-of-file marker is encountered.

Therefore, the file (when dumped) would start out with a block of data that looks like this:

```
31 20 43 55 42 45 20 20 20 20 20 20 20 20 20 20
20 20 20 20 20 20 20 20 20 20 20 20 20 20 20 20
20 20 20 20 20 20 20 20 20 20 20 20 20 20 20 20
20 20 20 20 20 20 20 20 20 20 20 20 20 20 20 20
20 20 20 20 20 20 20 20 20 20 20 20 20 20 20 20
```
(80 bytes with the words "1 CUBE").
```
0C 00 00 00
```
(number of facets = 12)
```
                  00 00 00 00 00 00 80 EF 72 04 35 31
```
(normal of first facet)
```
FF FF 3F 40 32 33 B3 3F FF FF 7F 40
```
(first vertex)
```
                                         FF FF 7F 40
32 33 B3 3F FF FF 7F 40
```
(second vertex)
```
                        FF FF 7F 40 32 33 B3 3F
FF FF 3F 40
```
(third vertex)
```
            00 00
```
(attribute bytes)

More facet descriptions would follow until the object is completely described.

Caveat

.STL files are created by the CAD program as another form of output or file translation — if available. Be advised that various sources report that .STL translators are not all created equal. Random facets may be unrepresented, leaving holes in the part, or facets may stick out into space, throwing the part out of tolerance. Normals may be flipped, and there may be stray vectors, producing "fuzz" on the surface of the part, requiring (at least) extra finishing. .STL files generated with surface-modeling CAD can be especially problematic, if only because the users are not accustomed to creating fully closed surfaces.

Because quarterly updates are a way of life, a CAD package may do the job differently from version to version. Getting user references and actually talking to those users may be the best move to make before investing in a CAD package for rapid automated prototyping.

CAD Programs With .STL Output

The following is a list of CAD or FEA packages or utilities that will produce .STL files, available in North America. The list is based on one supplied by 3D Systems, and can be expected to change over time. Listed is the package, the vendor, a phone number, the address if applicable, and the platform on which the software runs.

Advanced Visualizer
Wavefront Technologies Inc.
805-962-8117
530 E. Montecito St.
Santa Barbara, CA 93103
Silicon Graphics, HP, Sun, IBM RS/6000

Alias Studio or Designer
Alias Research Inc.
416-362-9181

110 Richmond St. East
Toronto, Canada, M5C 1P1
Silicon Graphics, IBM RS/6000

(.STL translator for Amiga CAD formats)
DFW Prototypes
817-275-2044
1920 Briar Crest Lane
Arlington, TX 76012
Amiga

Ansys
Mallet Software Tech Inc.
412-941-4201
4050 Washington Road
McMurray, PA 15317
Sun Microsystems

Aires Concept Station
Aires Technology Inc.
508-453-5310
600 Suffolk St.
Lowell, MA 01854
DEC, HP, Silicon Graphics, Sun, IBM RS/6000, SCO Open
    Desktop

AutoCAD
Autodesk Inc.
415-332-2344
2320 Marinship Way
Sausalito, CA 94965
DOS, Sun, Apple Macintosh

Bravo Solids
Applicon Inc. (Division of Schlumberger)
313-995-6000
4251 Plymouth Rd.
Ann Arbor, MI 48106-0986
DEC VAX, DEC Unix

CADAM ISD
CADAM Inc.
818-841-9470
1935 N. Buena Vista
Burbank, CA 91570
IBM RS/6000

CADKEY Version 5
CADKEY Inc.
203-298-8888
4 Griffin Road North
Windsor, CT 06095
DOS, Silicon Graphics, Sun, DEC

CADDS, Dimension III, Medusa
Computervision Corp.
617-275-1800
100 Crosby Drive
Bedford, MA 01730
Sun Microsystems, DEC, H-P

(.STL translators for ComputerVision CADDS, ComputerVision
    Personal Designer, and any IGES file)
Brock Rooney and Assoc.
313-645-0236
268 George St.
Birmingham, MI 48009
DOS, Sun Microsystems

Datasculpt®
Laser Design Inc.
612-884-9648
9401 James Avenue South #162
Minneapolis, MN 55431
DOS, Silicon Graphics

Sabre 5000
Gerber Systems Corp.
203-282-1478
83 Gerber St. East
South Windsor, CT 06074
Silicon Graphics, H-P

Hewlett-Packard ME30
Hewlett-Packard Corp.
800-752-0900
Unix

I/PROTOTYPE (Intergraph to .STL translator)
Intergraph Corp.
205-730-7539
Huntsville, AL 35894
Intergraph and Sun workstations

Modelmate Plus, Variametrix
Control Automation Inc.
407-676-3222
2350 Commerce Park Drive #4
Palm Bay, FL 32905
DOS (Modelmate), Sun (Variametrix)

(.STL translators for PDGS-Ford and IGES)
CTAD Systems Inc.
313-665-3287

3025 Broadwalk #175
Ann Arbor, MI 48108
Sun, IBM RS/6000, H-P, DEC, Unix

Pro Engineer
Parametric Technology Corp
617-894-7111
128 Technology Drive
Waltham, MA 02154
Sun, Silicon Graphics, DEC, H-P, IBM RS/6000, Unix

Microsolids Solid Modeler
Silicon Materials Inc.
412-367-3828
108 Ambleside Drive
Pittsburgh, PA 15237
DOS

(Cyberware scanner to .STL translator)
Solid Concepts Inc.
805-257-9300
26074 Avenue Hall #6
Valencia, CA 91355
(Cyberware systems)

Parasolids
EDS Unigraphics
314-344-5900
13736 Riverport Drive
St. Louis, MO 63043
DEC, HP, Sun, IBM RS/6000

SDRC I-DEAS
SDRC (Structural and Dynamics Research Corp.)
513-576-2400

2000 Eastman Drive

Milford, OH 45150

Apollo, H-P, DEC, Silicon Graphics, Sun, IBM RS/6000

SilverScreen

Schroff Development Corp.

913-262-2664

P.O. Box 1334

Mission, KS 66222

DOS

(.STL translator for Wavefront files)

The Post Group

213-462-2300

6335 Homewood Ave.

Hollywood, CA 90028

Sun, Silicon Graphics, Unix

Support Generator Software

As explained in Chapter 2, when building a stereolithography part, it is necessary to add supports that will keep it together during the building process. Islands that might float off, overhangs and unsupported areas that might sag or curl, adjacent profiles from which the unused resin might not drain, and downward facing sharp edges that might distort all need some sort of support.

You can add your own using the original CAD software, and that software may even include a "library" of supports. Or you can acquire support generator software that will do the job automatically, replacing hours of CAD work with 5 minutes of computer time. (The supports, usually webbing, columns, gussets and other projections, are thin enough to be peeled off by hand after curing.)

As this is written, only one vendor of support generator software was known, Solid Concepts.

SOLID CONCEPTS INC.

26075 Avenue Hall #6
Valencia, CA 91355
805-257-9300
fax: 805-257-9311

Solid Concepts offers two products: Bridgeworks, for support generation for the 3D SLA-190, the SLA-250, and the SLA-500, and SupSlice, which augments Bridgeworks on the SLA-500. (The firm is, incidentally, located across the street from 3D Systems.) Their support generator software has also been used with DTM wax selective laser sintering models to counteract heat distortion, and the firm is working to adapt their software to the Stratesys fused deposition model-making machine.

Bridgeworks

Platform: Silicon Graphics 4D, Sun SPARC, 386 PC, DECstation
    (IBM RS/6000 and Hewlett-Packard HP-700 planned)
Price: $4,995.00

Bridgeworks analyzes an .STL file and creates a new, second .STL file with the supports. About 95 percent of the time (the firm says) no further operator intervention is needed — the defaults work fine. An .STL to IGES converter, or the CAD program's reverse .STL converter, can be used to view the supports, although this is said to be rarely necessary.

The Bridgeworks software does not comprehend the part the way a person looking at it would but instead follows rules to make sure that all parts that need support are supported. It also tries to use the minimum number of supports for the job. If problems are encountered, many parameters can be changed by the operator, such as gusset spacing, gusset thickness, gusset length and gusset angle, webbing and column thicknesses, maximum overhangs and slopes that should be supported, the slicing axis, and more.

SupSlice
Platforms: Silicon Graphics 4D, 386 PC
Price: $1,000.00

SupSlice optimizes Bridgeworks for the SLA-500, replacing 3D's slicing software and eliminating cobwebbing of supports and other problems. Colinear vectors are combined to reduce vector count and the size of the slice file, by up to 50 percent.

Glossary

Alpha-numeric. Data in the form of numerals and alphabetical characters — basically, anything that could be produced from a keyboard. As opposed to graphical data, which involves arrays of pixels, and numeric values encoded as binary numbers.

ASCII. American Standard Code for Information Interchange, the character code used by computers (except IBM mainframes and a few other special cases) to represent alphabetic characters and numerals. There are two versions, seven-bit ANSI (American National Standards Institute) ASCII with 128 characters, including control characters and all the characters on the PC keyboard; and nonstandard eight-bit ASCII with the ANSI ASCII characters and an extra 128 more — usually special purpose, foreign, and graphical characters.

B-Spline. A mathematical representation of a smooth curve.

Bit. A single binary integer — a single one or a single zero.

Binary. (1) The representation of data through a coding that uses only ones and zeroes, as done in computers. (2) File format in which the data is represented as binary numbers (although often rendered by the computer as hexadecimal values), as opposed to ASCII format, where the data is in human-readable alpha-numeric characters.

Byte. Eight binary integers, handled by the computer as one data unit, used to represent a single alpha-numeric character. Other data types may require more than one byte per item.

C. Programming language often used by professionals for commercial projects. Recent variants include C++ (pronounced "sea plus plus").

CAD. Computer-Aided Design. Also called CADD, Computer-Aided Design and Drafting.

CAD/CAM. Computer-Aided Design, Computer-Aided Manufacturing. The linking of CAD and CAM files with any automated industrial process.

CAE. Computer-Aided Engineering, the use of software to conduct engineering-related analytical tasks.

CALS. Computer-Aided Acquisition and Logistics Support. A set of standards chosen by the Department of Defense to achieve paperless documentation. (There is an office in the Detroit area that produces about 60,000 new prepress pages a year of paper documentation, just for the U.S. Army tank corps.) Included among the standards are CGM, IGES, MIL-STD 1840A, and SGML.

CAM. Computer-Aided Manufacturing, which includes NC machines, robotics, shop floor tracking, and other factory computer applications.

CASE. Computer-Aided Software Engineering — generally, the use of software to ease the creation of software.

CGM. Computer Graphics Metafile. A cross-platform graphics interchange standard using both vector and raster descriptions.

Compatibility. Refers to the ability of hardware and software to work together, regardless of their origins.

Crash. The complete failure of a computer system, usually by locking and ignoring further input. A software crash (the commonest kind) can usually be rectified by rebooting. A disk crash (rarer) may require the replacement of hardware.

Cured Strength. The strength of a finished stereolithography part, after it has emerged from the model-making machine and been subjected to curing, either by heat or a UV floodlight.

Cursor. The flashing spot on the screen where impending screen activity will take place.

DOS. Disk Operating System, usually for the PC, and can stand for MS-DOS from Microsoft, PC-DOS from IBM, and DR DOS from Digital Research. Application software intended for DOS should run on either.

Drawing. CAD (or other) graphic rendering of an object via a two-dimensional view or associated multiple views, with dimensions, labels, and other notations. Unlike a CAD model, a CAD drawing cannot be subjected to computerized structural analysis and is unsuited for rapid automated prototyping.

.DXF. The external drawing exchange file format used by Autodesk's AutoCAD and widely used by other CAD vendors.

FDM. Fused Deposition Modeling, the model-making method used by Stratasys Inc.

FEA. Finite Element Analysis, the computer-aided structural, thermal, and magnetic analysis of an object.

Green Strength. The strength of a stereolithography part after it emerges from the model-making machine but before it is cured, either by exposure to heat or a UV floodlamp.

GUI. Graphical User Interface, pronounced "gooey," such as Microsoft Windows and the Apple Macintosh interface.

Hard Tooling. To make casting dies out of steel for full-scale production of end-user items.

Hexadecimal. The base-16 number system, also called hex, commonly used to represent binary numbers, since, for instance, 12C (hex) is easier to write then 100101100 (binary), but it means 300 (decimal). Similarly, 640k (the limit of conventional memory in a PC) is really 655,360 but is A0000 in hex. The hexadecimal numbers run 1 through F (15), and, then, 16 is 10.

IGES. Initial Graphic Exchange Specification. A nonproprietary graphics exchange standard generally used for CAD documents, defined by ANSI standard Y14.28.

Investment Casting. Also called lost wax casting. A wax prototype is surrounded by mold material. After the mold hardens, the wax is melted and poured out. Production material can then be poured into the void thus created, replicating the original model with new material.

K. Numerical suffix, meaning either 1,000 (as in salaries, 60K = $60,000) or 1,024 (in computer science, being two raised to the tenth power, so that 640K = 655,360 bytes.)

Kilobytes. Bytes measured in increments of 1,024.

LAN. Local Area Network — an arrangement whereby computers can share each other's disk files and other peripherals, usually through coaxial cable or some other method of direct connection.

LOM. Laminated Object Manufacturing, the model-making method used by Helisys Inc.

M. In computer science, M means million, not thousand.

Megabyte. 1,048,576 bytes (i.e., a thousand kilobytes).

MIL-STD 1840A. An interchange standard for files stored on magnetic tape, part of the CALS specification.

NC. Numerical Control, refers to computer-controlled milling and cutting machines used in conventional model-making.

NURB or NURBS. Non-Uniform Rational B-Splines, a common method of ensuring "homogenous geometry" in CAD representations — meaning that all points, lines, surfaces, etc., share a common mathematical form and can all be manipulated and edited with the same routines.

NVP. N-vinyl pyrrolidone, also rendered 1-vinyl-2-pyrrolidinone, or N-vinyl-2-pyrrolidone, a compound used as a diluent in some stereolithography photoactive polymer resins. Ciba-Geigy's data sheet warns: "Suspected of cancer hazard. Causes severe eye irritation. Causes skin irritation and possible allergic skin reaction. Harmful if inhaled. Harmful if swallowed. Repeated overexposure can cause central nervous depression, nausea, vomiting, and may cause liver damage. Avoid contact with eyes, skin and clothing. Wear eye protection and impervious gloves when handling. Wash thoroughly after handling. Avoid breathing vapor or mist. Keep container closed when not in use. Use only with adequate ventilation. Do not take internally. Fully cured plastic parts are no longer hazardous. Nuisance dust may be generated when sanding or sawing cured material. Avoid breathing dust."

Operating System. The basic software that controls the computer and serves as the intermediary between the application software and the computer. It may be considered part of the computer, since the computer is useless without it. Common examples are MS-DOS and Unix.

PC. A microcomputer based on the Intel 8080 chip set and its later derivatives (i.e., the 8086, 80286, 80386, 80486, etc.) that can run software written for the MS-DOS operating system. The "architecture" of the PC was defined by the original IBM PC that came out in 1981, but it is now cloned by hundreds of vendors — which is legal, as long as they do not copy the IBM PC ROM BIOS.

SGC. Solid Ground Curing, the approach to stereolithography used by Cubital, whereby each layer of the model is cured and milled before the next one is added.

SLA. Stereolithography Apparatus. Any model-making machine from 3D Systems.

Slice. To analyze a CAD file and render it as a successive pile of cross-sections that can be created by a model-making machine.

SLS. Selective laser sintering, the model-making technology used by DTM Corp.

Soft Tooling. The use of aluminum casting dies to make test items or short-run end-user items.

Solid Modeling. The most demanding and realistic approach to CAD, whereby parts are represented as three-dimensional objects rather than as associated two-dimensional views, or as wire-frame or surface modeling three-dimensional drawings. Solid modeling allows accurate structural analysis and is recommended for most forms of rapid automated prototyping. "Boundary representation" CAD stores the actual geometry of the object, while "constructive solid geometry" CAD stores Boolean equations from which the geometry is constructed.

Spline. A parametric polynomial curve whose points obey certain constraints — although often used simply to mean "curve."

.STL. The CAD file exchange format developed by 3D Systems for use with its stereolithography model-making machines, and widely used throughout the field of rapid automated prototyping. See Chapter 7 for details.

Surface Modeling. The computer rendering of a three-dimensional object in which the surfaces are shaded. Unlike solid modeling, surface modeling can be used to create impossible objects, since a collection of surfaces does not have to conform to the rules of the real world.

Ultraviolet or UV. Nonvisible light with wavelenghts immediately below the purple end of the visible spectrum (about 4,000 angstroms) to the border of the x-ray region (about 40 angstroms). Most UV in sunlight is supposed to be filtered out by the Earth's atmospheric ozone layer.

Unix. Also written UNIX. An operating system, originated by AT&T, designed for multi-user systems, with built-in telecommunications functions. It is popular mostly in the academic and scientific communities, and for use on workstations of the kind often used for CAD. Unfortunately, there are about 25 different versions.

Windows. (1) A graphical user interface for the PC, from Microsoft. Runs with DOS, although the future version will probably embody its own operating system. (2) Generically, the presentation of information or options on a screen so that when the presentation disappears the original appearance of the screen will be restored.

Wire Frame Modeling. The computer rendering of a three-dimensional object in which only the edges or boundaries are represented — you can "see through" the surfaces.

Workstation. A high-end single-user computer, usually with a graphical user interface and networking functionality, often running under Unix, used for sophisticated engineering and CAD work.

X-Windows. A graphical user interface for Unix environments, similar to, but not compatible with, Microsoft Windows.

Index